NETHERLAND BY JOSEPH O'NEILL

&

PRESIDENT BARAK OBAMA'S

AMERICA

A HISTORICAL-LITERARY EXAMINATION

Hermit Kingdom Studies in Identity and Society, 2

Netherland by Joseph O'Neill
&
President Barak Obama's
AMERICA
A Historical-Literary Examination

Heerak Christian Kim

The Hermit Kingdom Press
Highland Park * Seoul * Bangalore * Cebu

Netherland by Joseph O'Neill & President Barak Obama's AMERICA:
A Historical-Literary Examination
(Hermit Kingdom Studies in Identity and Society, 2)

Copyright ©2010 Heerak Christian Kim

All rights reserved. No part of this book may be reproduced in any form or by any means, electronic or mechanical, including photocopying, recording, or by any information storage and retrieval system (including computer files in any form), without permission in writing from the publisher.

Hardcover ISBN13: 978-1-59689-094-7
Paperback ISBN13: 978-1-59689-096-1

ISSN: 1932-6726

Write To Address:
The Hermit Kingdom Press
P. O. Box 1226
Highland Park, NJ 08904-1226
The United States of America

Library of Congress Cataloging-in-Publication Data

Kim, H. C. (Heerak Christian)
 Netherland by Joseph O'Neill & President Barack Obama's America : a historical-literary examination / Heerak Christian Kim.
   p. cm. -- (Hermit Kingdom studies in identity and society ; 2)
 ISBN 978-1-59689-094-7 (hardcover : alk. paper) -- ISBN 978-1-59689-096-1 (pbk. : alk. paper)
 1. O'Neill, James, 1909-1973. Netherland. 2. National characteristics, American, in literature. 3. Politics and literature--United States--History--21st century. 4. Literature and society--United States--History--21st century. I. Title.
 PR6065.N435N4835 2010
 823'.914--dc22
                        2010021947

Table of Contents

"Netherland and American Militarism" / page 1

"Chuck Ramkissoon and the History and Character of Trinidad" / page 23

"Abelsky and Shylock the Jew" /page 94

Netherland by Joseph O'Neill & President Barak Obama's AMERICA

"Netherland and American Militarism"[1]

In many ways, Barack Obama's rise to the Presidency of the United States of America can be seen as a Shreck-like fairytale story come true. Barack Obama described his African father as "black as pitch" and his Kansas mother as "white as milk" and recounted in his memoir, *Dreams from My Father: A Story of Race and Inheritance*, his personal and psychological journey, struggling with his biracial identity, including his teenager desire to renounce his mother's race in order not to ingratiate himself to whites.[2] From his teenage years, Barack Obama made a personal journey that resulted in the decision to run for the US Presidency. However, even as late as January 22, 2006, Barack Obama claimed that he was not seeking to become the President or the Vice President when Tim Russert asked him. However, ten months later, when Tim Russert asked him again during NBC's *Meet the Press*, Obama said that it is fair to say that he is thinking about running for President in 2008.[3] On March 4, 2007, in Selma, Alabama, Barack Obama faced Hillary Clinton for the first time since he and Hillary Clinton

---

[1] This chapter represents expansion of the academic paper delivered at the Annual Midwest American Academy of Religion (AAR) conference meeting, held in Augustana College, Rock Island, Illinois, in March, 2010. I would like to thank Professor Kristin Schwain of the Department of Art History and Archaeology of the University of Missouri, who chaired the Art, Literature, and Religion section, where the academic paper was presented, for her support and helpful comments.
[2] Dan Balz and Haynes Johnson, *The Battle for America 2008: The Story of an Extraordinary Election* (New York: Viking, 2009), p. 4.
[3] Balz and Johnson, *The Battle for America 2008*, pp. 17-18.

announced their campaigns for the White House.[4] At first, it seemed like Barack Obama had no chance for victory. Dan Balz and Haynes Johnson describe Hillary Clinton's advantage: "She is the best known, has the most formidable political organization, the most money, the greatest expertise. She's backed by a network that has helped win the White House twice, something no Democrat had accomplished since FDR, and can recruit almost anyone she wants."[5] But Barack Obama beat Hillary Clinton. And Barack Obama went on to beat the Republican candidate.

The question is why? Why was Barack Obama able capture the majority of the American people's support to win the White House? Why did Barack Obama become so popular? The answer can be found in American people's growing opposition to the War on Terror.[6] From the very beginning, Barack Obama made it clear that he opposed the War on Terror. In fact, Barack Obama opposed attacking Saddam Hussein and invading Iraq.

At an anti-Iraq war rally in Chicago, Barack Obama said, "I know that Saddam poses no imminent and direct threat to the United States or to his neighbors, that the Iraqi economy is in shambles, that the Iraq military is a fraction of its former strength, and that in concert with the international community he can be contained until, in the way of all petty dictators, he falls away into the dustbin of history."[7] Barack Obama was unequivocal about his opposition to attacking Saddam Hussein

---

[4] Balz and Johnson, *The Battle for America 2008*, p. 3.
[5] Balz and Johnson, *The Battle for America 2008*, p. 4.
[6] Colleen Elizabeth Kelley notes: "As of July 8, 2007, the official death count for Americans killed in Iraq since the war began was 3,606, most of whom have died since President George W. Bush made his May 1, 2003, declaration of victory and 'mission accomplished.' The official count of Americans wounded was 25,558 with estimates running as high as 100,000" (Colleen Elizabeth Kelley, *Post-9/11 American Presidential Rhetoric: A Study of Protofascist Discourse* {Lanham: Lexington Books, 2007}, p. 2).
[7] Balz and Johnson, *The Battle for America 2008*, p. 22.

or making a military-spurred regime change in Iraq. In his political speech to declare publicly his position on War on Terror, Barack Obama stood against not only President George W. Bush, but also the US Congress which supported the War on Terror.

Furthermore, Barack Obama painted all those who supported the War on Terror and in particular the Bush War in Iraq as ideologically driven without regard for American domestic wellbeing or the welfare of the poor in the world.[8] Barack Obama said at the rally, "What I am opposed to is the cynical attempt by Richard Perle and Paul Wolfowitz and other arm chair weekend warriors in this administration to shove their own ideological agendas down our throats, irrespective of the costs in lives lost and in hardship borne."[9] Thus, Barack Obama argued, in essence, that the Bush Administration was waging a war that violated human rights and civil rights.[10]

---

[8] Kelley notes: "The number of Iraqi civilians dead because of the war is less precise. It ranges from 'low-end' military estimate of between 66,939 and 73,253 to more than 650,000 dead according to a study released by the British medical journal *Lancet* (Kelley, *Post-9/11 American Presidential Rhetoric*, p. 2). That is far more than Saddam Hussein is accused of killing.

[9] Balz and Johnson, *The Battle for America 2008*, p. 21.

[10] It must be noted that many Americans view the War on Terror as essentially violating American civil rights as well. Kelley notes: "By 2004, Unitarian minister Davidson Loehr was warning that, unless there is an intervention, the future of the United States was sober and decidedly un-democratic. In this view, civil liberties would continue to diminish, a necessary condition 'for fascism to work,' while media such as National Public Radio and the Public Broadcasting System, which occasionally question the status quo or reigning administration, will lose funding as they are 'enemies of the state's official stories.' In addition there would likely be less free speech and more national security accompanied by a tighter control of editorial bias and 'demonization of the few media' still uncontrolled as well as criminalization of those who protest such moves on the part of the government as 'un-American, with arrests, detentions and harassment increasing.' …. The president's defenders argue that post-9/11 'war-

Netherland by Joseph O'Neill & President Barak Obama's AMERICA

The US Congress that supported the war was implicated in the guilt as well by association, including Senator Hillary Clinton. The 11-page, single-spaced memo entitled "Launch Strategy Thoughts" by Mark Penn to Hillary Clinton, shortly before Christmas 2006, "concluded by addressing the issue that most threatened her hopes of winning the nomination: Her support for the resolution authorizing Bush to go to war in Iraq had created a breach with the left in the Democratic Party – and an opening for Obama."[11] Ironically, the anti-War on Terror position is what propelled Barack Obama from a virtual unknown to become the victorious candidate for the office of the US President in 2008.

It is important to note that John McCann lost the Presidency because he espoused President George W. Bush's War on Terror and pushed aggressive American militarism. Although he started to prepare for the 2008 Presidential race much earlier, John McCann took a tactic that went against the anti-war sentiment of the American people, both Republicans and Democrats. John McCann said, like a paranoid, scared POW, "The consequences of failure are immense. ... If we leave Iraq, if you read Zarqawi, bin Laden, all of these other terrorists, they're not going to just be satisfied with Iraq. They're coming after us."[12] The fear that John McCann had toward backward, technologically deficient terrorists who sprouted mere rhetoric seemed strange to the American people who knew how strong the US military might is. It made the Republican Party look ridiculous and weak, and in contrast, Barack Obama and anti-war Democrats looked cool and above fear and destabilizing paranoia produced by War on Terror.

That is why the American people, both Republican[13] and Democrat, voted Barack Obama in as the US President and

---

time' conditions justify his actions" (Kelley, *Post-9/11 American Presidential Rhetoric*, p. 264).

[11] Balz and Johnson, *The Battle for America 2008*, p. 52.

[12] Balz and Johnson, *The Battle for America 2008*, p. 40.

[13] Balz and Johnson notes: "To a startling degree, Democrats, Republicans, and Independents, liberals, moderates, and

delivered the Congress solidly into Democrat hands. Barack Obama struck a key cord in the *zeitgeist* of the American people.[14]

The Annenberg Public Center of the University of Pennsylvania, under the guidance of the pollster Peter Hart, conducted ten focus groups, starting the spring of 2007, nine months from the first primary, and continuing throughout the primaries and election campaigns.

The first group of Republicans, Democrats, and Independents showed that nearly everyone had problems with the War in Iraq. Balz and Johnson describes: "At that point, the Iraq war was *the* dominant issue, one that darkened nearly everyone's opinion about America, regardless of political leaning. Republicans who had supported George W. Bush and Democrats who had opposed him agreed that U.S. policy toward Iraq was not working and needed to be changed."[15] John McCann and the Republican Party machine were completely blind to their own Republican Party members' desires. Certainly, it was primarily Barack Obama's anti-War on Terror position that garnered the votes from both Republicans

---

conservatives agreed about the troubled state of the nation, no matter their disagreement over policies and political personalities, their regions and individual backgrounds. These voters were eager, almost desperate, to 'turn the page,' as Barack Obama's call for fundamental change put it – and they needed to rally behind a candidate who offered the best hope of delivering on that promise" (Balz and Johnson, *The Battle for America 2008*, p. 57).

[14] Americans feared the aggrandizement of presidential powers. For example, since President Bush, the Executive Branch has been usurping the rights of the free press. Kelley notes: "There are several examples of its 'assault' on the press freedoms. They include infiltrating public broadcasting, manufacturing 'fake' news releases, bribing journalists, lying about the Iraq War, eliminating dissent in the mainstream media, 'gutting' the Freedom of Information Act, and consolidating media control" (Kelley, *Post-9/11 American Presidential Rhetoric*, pp. 270-271). Unfortunately, it seems like President Obama is continuing President Bush's legacy.

[15] Balz and Johnson, *The Battle for America 2008*, p. 58.

and Democrats. Thus, Obama became the most popular candidate in America. But all changed as President Barack Obama took up Bush's War on Terror.

On October 8, 2009, CNN poll asked the question: "Has President Obama's honeymoon ended?" Among the respondents, 44% responded, "Yes." And 42% answered with a question, "What honeymoon?" Thus, 86% of those who responded agree that President Obama is not liked, currently.[16]

---

[16] This is particularly significant in light of almost unanimous support of African-Americans for Obama's presidency. Jabari Asim describes his mother's near deification of Obama: "When I visited my mother last May, much of her living room had been converted into what I half jokingly called a Barack Obama shrine. Since Obama had declared his candidacy for president, my mother had diligently collected everything about the man that she could get her hands on. Magazines, newspaper articles, and T-shirts formed the bulk of her collection, all of it in pristine condition and not to be handled except with utmost care. Almost overnight, all things Obama had become a staple of my mother's conversation" (Jabari Asim, *What Obama Means ... for Our Culture, Our Politics, Our Future* {New York: William Morrow, 2009}, p. 1). Jabari Asim's description of his mother reveals a general sentiment among the African-Americans in realizing a president who is African-American. Obama represents realization of hope for the African-American community and African-American individuals. Thus, there is almost a blind support for Obama among the African-American communities, and that may explain relative silence among African-American intellectuals and politicians regarding Obama's continuance of Bush's War on Terror. This is not surprising form a sociological perspective because for many African-Americans, Obama represents a type of conversion experience. Jabari Assim describes his mother even changing her phone greeting as the result of Obama: "Instead of her usual 'Hello,' she took to lifting the receiver and announcing, 'This is our moment'" (Asim, *What Obama Means*, p. 2). The "our" referred to "African-American." The support for Obama was not merely among old African-Americans. In fact, young African-Americans were aggressive in supporting Obama. One such example is Jay-Z, perhaps the most famous rapper of today, who aggressively supported Obama during his concert tours. Asim describes: "Jay-Z, who offered vocal support of

Netherland by Joseph O'Neill & President Barak Obama's AMERICA

A part of the reason for the American dislike of President Obama is what Americans perceives as his administration's aggressive militarism in the Middle East, raising the number of

---

Obama during stops on his 2007 concert tour, … told *Vibe* magazine, 'So in the concert, I always say, "This is not sponsored by Obama." I make it very clear to say that, 'cause I know – "Obama associated with this guy from f-in' Marcy projects?!" I know that's coming any day. I think about that often. I mean, what do you do? What do I do? I have to support the guy…. But I don't wanna hurt him. I ain't like the preachers and all those guys'" (Asim, *What Obama Means*, p. 41). Thus, a famous African-American musician was willing to debase himself to protect Obama, whom he did not know personally, just because Obama was an African-American running for the office of US President. Jay-Z was not alone in his aggressive support of Obama. Asim describes: "But the clear message coming from many rap artists leading up to the election was one of unqualified support. 'what [Obama] represents is, we as a people are a part of the American Dream,' Jay-Z said. 'The message is for a kid from Marcy projects right now to say, "Maybe I can be the president."' Nas, Jay-Z's onetime rival and a rapper not known for his enthusiastic support of electoral politics, also weighed in. The chorus of his song, 'Black President' incorporated Obama's 'yes we can' mantra, while his lyrics concluded, 'I'm thinkin' I can trust this brotha.' …. Big Boi, one-half of Outkast, a Grammy-winning duo from Atlanta, presented a compelling slice of working-class life in a music video dedicated to Obama. In 'Something's Gotta Give,' Big Boi rapped about trying to find 'a righteous path' while inviting strangers he met on the street to volunteer at an Obama campaign office. …. Young Jeezy told MTV News. 'Listen to what he's saying: He's saying what I wanna hear … I'mma go vote for him. I can vote, by the way. Watch me, I'm going to register to vote. His song 'My President' included what was probably the earthiest rendition of Obama's signature phrase. 'We ready for damn change,' Jeezy declared, 'so y'all let the man shine.' Despite the occasional misfire, such as Ludacris's mixtape wishing paralysis on John McCain, the hip-hop community was overwhelmingly supportive of Obama's campaign" (Asim, *What Obama Means*, pp. 42-43). Thus, in light of near unanimous support for Obama in the African-American community, the statistics showing Obama's unpopularity is particularly significant.

troops in Afghanistan and increasing military incursions in Afghanistan and Pakistan. Many Americans believe that the aggressive American militarism is immoral and feel a moral or religious obligation to oppose it.[17] This sentiment is encapsulated in Lorraine Besser-Jones' statement: "Perhaps unsurprisingly, I argue that just war theory must condemn the war on terror."[18]

This sentiment of the American people is best identified in the popularity of Joseph O'Neill's book, *Netherland*, which takes an aggressive position against US militarism in the character of Rachel, the wife of the protagonist Hans van den Broek. Not only is this book, published in 2008, a national bestseller in the United States, it has garnered many prestigious American literary awards, such as The Pen/Faulkner Award. The New York Times identified this book as the best book of the year.

Even President Obama, before he became the President, when he was taking an aggressive anti-Iraq war position, called this book, "Fascinating...a wonderful book." It is this book's aggressive hostility to American militarism in the Middle East that has made this book a critical and popular

---

[17] There is even the question of who is a "terrorist." Simon Keller, thus, states: "The second reason why there shouldn't be a war on terrorism is that there are too many hazards associated with real-world judgments about who is and who is not a terrorist. It is often difficult to say whether or not a particular group is engaged in terrorism, and often easy to make people believe that a particular group is engaged in terrorism, even if it isn't..." (Simon Keller, "On What Is the War on Terror?" in Timothy Shanahan (ed.), *Philosophy 9/11: Thinking about the War on Terrorism* {Chicago: Open Court, 2005, pp. 53-68}, p. 67). In other words, many people can suffer unjustly as the result of wrongly labeling an individual or a group as "terrorist," whether by intention or by accident.

[18] Lorraine Besser-Jones, "Just War Theory, Legitimate Authority, and the 'War' on Terror" in Timothy Shanahan (ed.), *Philosophy 9/11: Thinking about the War on Terrorism* {Chicago: Open Court, 2005, pp. 129-148}, p. 130).

success. Many Americans feel that the War in Iraq/Afghanistan is immoral and unethical, and the book's critical and popular success is a testimony of this zeitgeist of the American people.

Currently, many high schools require their students to read this book as a part of their English class, which further highlights the negative sentiment of American educators and high school teachers regarding America's aggressive militarism in the Middle East. In the book, Rachel says in criticism of American militarism, "Bush wants to attack Iraq as part of a right-wing plan to destroy international law and order as we know it and replace it with the global rule of American force. Tell me which part of that sentence is wrong, and why." This didactic demonization of American militarism in the Middle East is a part of the book's position that it is moral and ethical to oppose America or boycott America. The main characters, Hans and Rachel, return back to England, and the ending of the book highlights the destruction of the American dream in the idea, "Violence begets violence." This US national bestseller is a testimony to the underlying zeitgeist of the American people.

The book obviously associates former US President George W. Bush[19] with American militarism, but the rhetoric could just as equally be applied to current US President Barak Obama, who is following the militarism of President Bush.[20]

---

[19] Carl Pedersen argues that George W. Bush marked the end of the "Next American Century" that began from the fall of the Berlin Wall in 1989. It was preceded by the short American century from the overthrow of Hawaii in 1893 to the fall of the Berlin Wall in 1989. Pedersen argues that Obama marks the "Post-American Century," in which will be obligated to share power with a host of rising powers, "both state and non-state" (Carl Pedersen, *Obama's America* {Edinburgh: Edinburgh University Press, 2009}, p. 125). In other words, Obama marks the end of American dominance in the world.

[20] It cannot be gainsaid that President Barack Obama is following in the footsteps of President George W. Bush, who conceived American military activity in Iraq and Afghanistan as an integral part of the global War on Terror. Ian S. Lustick states: "As I have stressed, the [Bush] administration has urged the country to share its view of the

After all, President Obama reappointed President Bush's Defense Secretary, Robert Gates. Interestingly enough, President Obama is continuing the Bush's War in Afghanistan with Bush's Defense Secretary. This means that whatever problems Bush's War in Afghanistan spurred is also instigated by President Obama and Obama's War in Afghanistan. Douglas Kellner points out the problem of the War in Afghanistan:

> The Bush administration and Pentagon policies in the Afghanistan war were poorly conceived, badly executed, and are likely to sow the seeds of future blowback and reprisal. Hence, although the overthrow of the Taliban regime and the assault on the Al Qaeda infrastructure were arguably justifiable and a salutary blow against global terrorism, the Bush administration and Pentagon's campaign in Afghanistan was arguably misconceived and, in many ways, unsuccessful. Terrorism is a global problem that requires a global solution. The Bush administration's policy, however, is largely unilateral; its military response is flawed and has hindered more intelligent and potentially successful efforts against terror networks, while quite possibly creating more terrorists and enemies of the United States.[21]

---

wars in Afghanistan and Iraq as integral parts of the global War on Terror. …. In an independent analysis of the current, long-term, direct, and indirect costs of the Iraq war, Nobel Prize-winning economist Joseph E. Stiglitz and Harvard scholar Linda Bilmes concluded that the total costs of the war, compared with costs incurred by the U.S. government had the war not been launched, would probably be more than $2 trillion" (Ian S. Lustick, *Trapped in the War on Terror* {Philadelphia: University of Pennsylvania Press, 2006}, p. 23).

[21] Douglas Kellner, *From 9/11 to Terror War: The Dangers of the Bush Legacy* (Lanham: Rowman & Littlefield Publishers, Inc., 2003), p. 2.

Obama seems to be continuing the fruitless and doomed War in Afghanistan, taking up Bush's war.

Thus, *The Economist* notes: "Anti-war activists, who rallied round him in the Democratic primaries because he was the only top-tier candidate to have opposed the Iraq war from the outset, now see worrying signs that their hero is a closet hawk."[22] Thus, it appears that Obama is at heart more like Bush with a policy similar to the policy of Bush.[23] Charlie Savage of New York Times states in his February 17, 2009, article, entitled, "Obama's War on Terror May Resemble Bush's in Some Areas": "Even as it pulls back from harsh interrogations and other sharply debated aspects of George W. Bush's 'war on terrorism,' the Obama administration is quietly signaling continued support for other major elements of its predecessor's approach to fighting Al Qaeda."[24]

Michael Hirsh of Newsweek, in fact, notes on February 21, 2008, that Obama had held to this war philosophy as the US Senator from Illinois, albeit silently: "And his 'comprehensive strategy' for that war, while it calls for 'getting out of Iraq and onto the right battlefield in Afghanistan and Pakistan,' still implies that the Illinois senator believes the war on terror should be the overarching framework for his foreign policy."[25]

---

[22] "Betrayed by Obama: Some of the New President's Arden Supporters Already Feel Let Down." *The Economist*. January 22, 2009 (http://www.economist.com/world/united-states/displaystory.cfm?story_id=E1_TNJRSVDV)

[23] *The Economist* notes that it may be the pro-Zionist faction in Obama's administration that may help fuel Obama's militarism: "John Pilger, an Australian journalist, bristles that the vice-president, Joe Biden, is 'a proud war-maker and Zionist', while Mr Obama's chief of staff, Rahm Emanuel, is a Zionist who 'opposes meaningful justice for the Palestinians.'" ("Betrayed by Obama" http://www.economist.com/world/united-states/displaystory.cfm?story_id=E1_TNJRSVDV)

[24] http://www.nytimes.com/2009/02/18/us/politics/18policy.html

[25] http://www.newsweek.com/id/114385

In other words, Barack Obama used the "anti-war position" merely to in a political victory against his establishment opponents. Thus, it is not surprising that while getting rid of the term "War on Terror", Obama is carrying out a war on terror, in fact.[26]

In fact, Joe Klein in *Time* magazine calls the War in Afghanistan, "Obama's War."[27] Regarding President Obama ordering 30,000 more troops to Afghanistan, Joe Klein states: "The President made the best possible argument for a rather iffy proposition: the expansion of a war that is 51% necessary and 49% futile (or vice versa). But you can't argue a people into war, especially one that seems so indistinct and perplexing."[28] Certainly, Klein points out the meaninglessness of the War in Afghanistan. Klein blatantly states the American sentiment about President Obama's militarism: "There are those, especially in the Democratic Party, who find such romanticism delusional and obscene; it rankles particularly when applied to a questionable war."[29]

---

[26] It is ironic that Barack Obama, who won on anti-war platform, should embrace the policy of George W. Bush. Ronald A. Faucheux notes that Obama's anti-war position even brought many financial supporters which allowed him to win against Hillary Clinton and eventually against the Republicans. Faucheux states: "Obama's change message, his anti-Iraq war position, his appeal to the young and well-educated, and his support among liberal 'netroots' activists and contributors were all tailor-made for a robust small-donor fundraising operation that relied heavily on Internet technology to harvest dollars" (Ronald A. Faucheux, "Why Clinton Lost" in Dennis W. Johnson (ed.), *Campaigning for President 2008: Strategy and Tactics, New Voices and New Techniques* {New York: Routledge, 2009, pp. 44-59}, p. 56). In fact, Faucheux argues that Hillary Clinton's vote in favor of the War in Iraq was a major contributing factor for why she lost the Democratic primaries to Obama (Faucheux, "Why Clinton Lost," p. 47).
[27] Joe Klein, "A President and His War," *Time* (Vol. 174, No. 23, December 14, 2009, pp. 36-40), p. 36.
[28] Klein, "A President and His War," p. 36.
[29] Klein, "A President and His War," p. 38.

Netherland by Joseph O'Neill & President Barak Obama's AMERICA

Time magazine, in fact, quotes President Obama as saying, "I am painfully aware that this is politically unpopular."[30] Even President Obama is keenly aware that the American people oppose American militarism in Afghanistan as a people. Hirsh points out the ridiculousness of the American war on terror: "Let's think about this for a moment. A small group of ragged America-haters, who had one lucky day of mass murder nearly seven years ago, will continue to define the foreign policy of the lone superpower for years, possibly decades to come. There's something wrong with this picture."[31]

Bush's and Obama's ridiculous war on terror is condemned in the novel, *Netherland*. Ed Smith notes: "This unhistorical dismissiveness, O'Neill implies, draws from the same well as Bush's inability to understand vast swaths of the globe, including whole religions and civilisations. How ironic, O'Neill suggests, that America, with its heritage as a cultural melting pot, should adopt so simplistic a foreign policy."[32] Obviously, the same blame would be placed on Obama.

In the words of Rachel, Han's wife, the author of the novel captures the zeitgeist of the American people. Rachel states: "I'm saying the U.S. has no moral or legal authority to wage this war" (p. 97). This particular statement is directed at the American war against Iraq. But this statement could just as well be directed against the American war in Afghanistan. This is evident in Rachel's statement: "Bush wants to attack Iraq as part of a right-wing plan to destroy international law and order as we know it and replace it with the global rule of American force. Tell me which part of that sentence is wrong and why" (p. 96). Charles Krauthammer, a columnist for *The Washington Post*, stated in *Foreign Affairs* a sentiment similar to Rachel's in

---

[30] Klein, "A President and His War," p. 38.
[31] http://www.newsweek.com/id/114385
[32] "Netherland by Joseph O'Neill," *The Times* (June 20, 2008, http://entertainment.timesonline.co.uk/tol/arts_and_entertainment/books/fiction/article4178788.ece)

the idea that America is bent on exerting its rule of force. Carl Pedersen describes Krauthammer's position:

> The end of the Cold War's bipolar world and threat of nuclear annihilation did not herald the coming of a peaceful, multipolar world order, according to Krauthammer. Quite the contrary. For the foreseeable future, the US was the "center of world power" in a "new strategic environment" where the threat of conflict, far from diminishing, would increase.[33]

This became an integral part of US government policy under President George H. W. Bush. The leaked Defense Planning Guide (DPG) in 1992 states the policy of the George H. W. Bush vis-à-vis maintaining American dominance in the world by maintaining "the mechanisms for deterring potential competitors from even aspiring to a larger regional or global role."[34] Pedersen notes:

> This draft, disavowed and revised in 1992, proved to be the blueprint for the neoconservative foreign policy strategy that was formulated in opposition to the Clinton administration after Bush's defeat in 1992 and became an integral part of the geopolitical vision of Bush's son after 2001. The idea of US preponderance contributed to the start in 2003 of what neoconservative Michael Ledeen called "the war to remake the world."[35]

Thus, Rachel in *Netherland* represents widespread understanding of the American bully factor in global affairs.

---

[33] Pedersen, *Obama's America*, p. 131.
[34] Pedersen, *Obama's America*, p. 132.
[35] Pedersen, *Obama's America*, pp. 132-33.

Zadie Smith comments regarding Rachel's statement: "During a snowstorm, Hans and Rachel have the argument everyone has."[36] In other words, Zadie Smith is arguing that "everyone" was blaming President Bush for the War on Terror that destroyed international peace. Thus, the war that America is waging against Iraq[37] is, in fact, a destructive force in the world, according to the novel. The status quo is that there is a type of international law and order, even if there is terrorism in the world and even if there are despots, like Saddam Hussein, in the world. The true evil, according to the novel, is not the few isolated terrorists who sometimes succeed or the lone despot[38] who crushes some dissidents, but the United States of America, which systematically destroys the global framework that holds the disparate nations[39] and governments together in a tenuous peace.[40]

---

[36] "Two Paths for the Novel," *The New York Review of Books* (Vol. 55, No. 18, November 20, 2008, http://www.nybooks.com/articles/22083)

[37] President George W. Bush's speech at West Point to the graduating cadets represents a shift in the US policy to unilateral preemptive action; this was a shift from the US Cold War policy of deterrence and containment (Pedersen, *Obama's America*, pp. 133-134).

[38] It could be argued that Saddam Hussein was a legitimate ruler, since his people did not make a concerted effort to take power away from him. In this light, US action against Iraq and Saddam Hussein can be seen as violating another nation's sovereignty and, therefore, illegal under international law and against the guiding principles of just war. Lorraine Besser-Jones states: "No matter how tyrannical a dictator, he will only have power to the extent that people around him defer to that power. .... When people continue to live and exist as subjects to an authority, they are granting that authority power over them. Being part of a common life made possible and/or governed by a given entity thus amounts to granting that entity authority (Besser-Jones, "Just War Theory," p. 143). In other words, Saddam Hussein had both *de facto* and *de jure* authority to rule in Iraq, and the American government violated international law by violating that legitimate authority.

[39] Douglas Kellner adds that the War in Afghanistan is alienating Arab nations, especially since the American government policy of nepotism

Colleen Elizabeth Kelley states that America is legitimizing lawless violence through its War on Terror and rhetoric associated with it. Kelley state: "In addition, reflective rhetoric legitimizes many elements of the terrorist worldview. The world *is* bipolar; the barbaric, subhuman nature of others legitimizes the use of violence against them; emotions should be acted upon; action is courageous and moral; and action is superior to communication."[41] In essence, the novel portrays the United States as the real peace-breaker and the creator of global suffering. This "conspiracy" was attributed to a right-wing plan.

Obviously, this novel was written before Barak Obama became president. Thus, the spirit of the attack of US policy in the Middle East must be seen as transferred to the Obama Administration, which may not be in name "conservative" or "right wing", but certainly it is so in spirit. The idea that some are mistaken and do not know their own "conservative" or

---

of Israel provides a lens for seeing the intentions of wars in the Middle East: "There is also a sense that U.S. is losing the struggle for the hearts and minds of Arabs and Muslims because of its bellicose nationalism, aggressive militarism, often uncritical support of Israel, and failure to improve relations with Muslim nations and peoples. .... In much of the Arab world, the United States is seen as the major supporter of Israel and the inability." (Kellner, *From 9/11 to Terror War*, p. 3).

[40] Jane Mayer argues that President George W. Bush's actions were also breaking of law and order in America. Mayer states: "The legal steps taken by the Bush Administration in its war against terrorism were a quantum leap beyond earlier blots on the country's history and traditions: more significant than John Adam's Alien and Sedition Acts, than the imprisonment of Americans of Japanese descent during World War II. Collectively, Arthur Schlesigner Jr. argued, the Bush Administration's extralegal counterterrorism program presented the most dramatic, sustained, and radical challenge to the rule of law in American history" (Jane Mayer, *The Dark Side: The Inside Story of How the War on Terror Turned into a War on American Ideals* {New York: Doubleday, 2008}, p. 8).

[41] Kelley, *Post-9/11 American Presidential Rhetoric*, p. 34.

"right wing" bent is emphasized by Rachel, who accuses her husband of being "conservative" without knowing it. Rachel states: "You are a conservative. What's so sad is you don't even know it" (p. 97). This accusation would apply to Obama and the Obama Administration on the basis of his administrating the war in the Middle East. This book functions as an indictment of Obama because this book, which was written as an attack against President George W. Bush is functionally an attack of President Barak Obama, because they stand for the same things, in essence, when it comes to militarism in the Middle East.

Thus, on the one level, America's militarism is condemned from the perspective of anti-colonialism.[42] America is engaging in these wars in the Middle East in order to enjoy the rule of American force. It is a type of being drunk with power that the novel condemns vis-à-vis the United States. America is a colonialist[43] power wanting to wield its power on the subjugated colonies. In a sense, America wants to recreate the world in its image, as is characteristic of colonialist powers. Colonialism destroys nativism and traditions particular to that nation. Values and worldview of that region becomes

---

[42] Pedersen argues that China is able to surpass the USA in global influence because it does not make ideological demands of the countries it helps. Pedersen states: "China provides yet another model for augmenting its power. By pursuing a course of trade and investment in second world countries without any demands for reform or improvement of human rights, it can eclipse American power" (Pedersen, *Obama's America*, p. 141).

[43] Phillip McReynolds describes how someone or some group can be labeled terrorist by a dominating group: "'Terrorism' can be defined in a number of ways. According to a relativist view, the difference between 'terrorist' and 'freedom fighters' depends wholly or largely upon one's sympathies with the people involved" (Phillip McReynolds, "Terrorism as a Technological Concept: How Low versus High Technology Defines Terrorism and Dictates Our Responses" in Timothy Shanahan (ed.), *Philosophy 9/11: Thinking about the War on Terrorism* {Chicago: Open Court, 2005, pp. 69-89}, p. 74).

overturned and even criminalized and replaced with the mores of the colonizing power.

On another level, the novel condemns war-mongering.[44] The novel takes the position that war is essentially destructive.[45] Thus, peace that exists could be destroyed by war. The world is not perfect, but the world can exist in a relative peace.[46] This relative peace can be destroyed by war. Because wars are violent, wars are destructive.[47] In other words, violence begets

---

[44] Pedersen doubts that Obama's shift of war in Iraq to war in Afghanistan will prove a success: "However, Obama's decision to shift the focus of US military operations from Iraq to Afghanistan-Pakistan, where the long war began in October 2001, may prove counterproductive. .... Along with Iraq, Afghanistan and Pakistan are failed states and it is far from certain that the deployment of more American troops in Afghanistan will help in establishing a cohesive state there" (Pedersen, *Obama's America*, p. 148).

[45] Andrew Fiala writes: "At protests and rallies aimed at dissuading the Bush administration from going to war in Iraq, a common sign read War Is Terrorism" (Andrew Fiala, "Defusing Fear: A Critical Response to the War on Terrorism" in Timothy Shanahan (ed.), *Philosophy 9/11: Thinking about the War on Terrorism* {Chicago: Open Court, 2005, pp. 93-105}, p. 93).

[46] When Barack Obama was a state senator of Illinois, he spoke against the war in Iraq as a "dumb war" driven by "ideological agenda," right after President George W. Bush put forward a resolution in October 2002 to attack Saddam Hussein in Iraq by US military force. Pedersen describes Obama's speech on October 2, 2002, to an anti-war group in Chicago: "He regarded the impending war in Iraq as a politically motivated war designed to distract the attention of the American people from pressing problems at home – social inequality and a looming economic depression" (Pedersen, *Obama's America*, p. 152). It is ironic that President Barack Obama is doing the same thing as Bush.

[47] Andrew Fiala accuses the American government of using terror tactics and argues that that has to be stopped. Fiala writes: "If we are concerned to eliminate terrorism, then we should also be concerned to eliminate war or at least to restrain the tendency of military strategists to see terror tactics as an option" (Fiala, "Defusing Fear," p. 93).

violence. And America symbolizes violence and aggression. In order to start and maintain the War on Terror, President Obama and President Bush try to link those whom they attack with al-Qaeda. Kelley explains:

> In 2004, despite the report of the bipartisan commission investigating 9/11 that it found "no credible evidence" that Iraq and al-Qaeda cooperated in attacks on Americans, President Bush and other top administration officials were nonetheless defending their claims of close ties between Iraq and al-Qaeda terrorists. Bush, Vice President Dick Cheney, and National Security Adviser Condoleeza Rice argued the administration's position in speeches and interviews. The administration distributed "talking points' to counter criticism that they had hyped the Iraq-al-Qaeda connection in the buildup to war with Iraq.[48]

Both President Bush and President Obama are guilty of grouping "terrorists" together in haphazard and general ways to justify their War on Terror. *Netherland* explains this habit of America to justify war and aggression by linking groups and nations to al-Qaeda. It is based on lack of respect for law and order, a sense that America is a lone superpower. Rachel states: "The United States is now the strongest military power in the world. It can and will do anything it wants. It has to be stopped" (p. 98).[49] Jane Mayer notes: "America became the first nation ever to authorize violations of the Geneva

---

[48] Kelley, *Post-9/11 American Presidential Rhetoric*, p. 47.

[49] Peter Beinart notes: "This epic faith in the U.S.'s military, economic and ideological power fueled Bush's decision to define the war on terrorism as the U.S. against the field" ("Shrinking the War on Terrorism," *Time* {Vol. 174, No. 23, December 14, 2009, pp. 42-45}, p. 43).

Conventions."[50] America's breaking of the Geneva Conventions illustrates the point that Rachel makes in the novel. The statement made in *Netherland* by Rachel, an English woman, is further significant because there were one million marchers against the War in Iraq, when Tony Blair was the Prime Minister. Rachel accurately captures the zeitgeist of the British masses against the war in the Middle East.

In a sense, Rachel is blaming the United States of America for the terrorism that is raging in the world. The underlying logic of the book is that because the United States of America uses Machiavellian tactics in the world as the lone superpower of the world that America is no longer a safe place. Thus, America has to be stopped from its aggressive militarism because global unrest is fed by America's persistent militarism in the Middle East.

To highlight America's warmongering nature, the book points out the nuclear reactor in India Point, New York, which is only 30 miles away from Westchester County, New York. The narrator describes the precarious situation of living near New York: "If something bad happened there, we were constantly being informed, the 'radioactive debris,' whatever this might be, was liable to rain down on us" (p. 23). Obviously, the nuclear plant is meant to highlight the nuclear policy of the United States of America and, by extension, militaristic philosophy of the US government. In a sense, the book is arguing that the US government placed its citizens in a precarious situation through its militarism in the Middle East[51] and that this was an extension of the "normative" US government policy throughout the generations.

To highlight the idea that those who live by the sword could die by the sword, the book portrays America in a situation

---

[50] Mayer, *The Dark Side*, p. 9.

[51] Beinart states: "The harsh truth is that the U.S. is significantly weaker in the Middle East now than it was in 2002. For close to a decade, our adversaries have not only survived our efforts to destroy them; they've also realized that conflict with the U.S. has its advantages" (Beinart, "Shrinking the War on Terrorism," p. 45).

that the death could come any time. This thought is placed into the narration of the protagonist Hans, who describes his life and his family's existence in vicarious terms with the residents of New York: "We were trying to understand, that is, whether we were in a preapocalyptic situation, like the European Jews in the thirties or the last citizens of Pompeii, or whether our situation was merely near-apocalyptic, like that of the Cold War inhabitants of New York, London, Washington, and, for that matter, Moscow" (p. 24). Obviously, what Hans means is that he was trying to ascertain whether immanent and certain death loomed before them or if just a threat of death (which does not get realized) loomed before them. Many of the East European Jews of 1930s were killed as were the residents of Pompeii, in contrast to the Cold War, which did not bring about many deaths. But neither situation is good, because the idea is that death through nuclear bombs during the Cold War was a real threat that could be delivered in reality in real time. Hans comparing his time, which in fact, is our current time, with death or possible death scenarios is meant to make the readers think about their predicament. The current residents of New York are, in fact, living in a "preapocalyptic" or "near-apocalyptic" period. Either one is bad because Hans is showing that New Yorkers will either actually die in large numbers or can realistically die in large numbers at any time at the push of a button. In other words, New Yorkers are living with death possibility every day.

    To illustrate why New Yorkers seem to ignore this reality, the book has Hans the protagonist ask his father-in-law about how it was like for him to live during the Cold War with the threat of a nuclear war hanging over them. Charles Bolton, the father-in-law, states: "I'm not sure I can be much use to you. One simply got on with it and hoped for the best. We weren't building bunkers in the garden or running for the hills, if that's what you mean" (p. 25). Charles Bolton seems to brush aside the possibility of death, like most New Yorkers do, now. Thus, there is a kind of warning by the book to New Yorkers: "You think that you are safe going about your business and ignoring the real possibility. That's what every generation does." Obviously, it is hard to ask someone who is killed in the holocaust to ask what they felt before their death, and the book does not bring that discussion. But, of course, the answer is by analogy. The Eastern European Jews probably went about their business, hoping for the best, in the 1930s, kind of assuming that they would not be killed, even though the imminent danger was there. In other words, the difference between two scenarios is that one actually happened and the other one did not, although the imminent threat existed for both. In a sense, therefore, the book is casting the fate of the New Yorkers on precarious chance. New Yorkers may all die through some nuclear explosion, either the one via the nuclear power plant in India Point or through a nuclear bomb.

The fact that the book does not mention the nuclear bomb can be seen as strategic on the part of the author. The author wanted to portray the United States government as evil and the "terrorists" as victims of American militarism. That is why the scenario of a nuclear blast is cast onto India Point, a creation of the US government. However, it must be mentioned that the possibility of a nuclear bomb explosion by terrorists is hinted at in the idea of a "dirty bomb." The narrator states: "Then there was the question of dirty bombs. Apparently any fool could build a dirty bomb and explode it in Manhattan" (p. 24). This quote makes it clear that even though the hint of terrorists using nuclear bomb is hinted at, it is not outright stated. Furthermore, the words "any fool" illustrate the author's desire to steer the impression away from the idea that terrorists are the real bad guys. The book is consistent in portraying the US government as evil and the terrorists as victims responding to US militarism. And this portion is no different in that portrayal.

Interestingly enough, the book in a sense argues with the strategic standpoint of America that the War on Terror is meant to be a war of deterrence, a policy that carried over from the Cold War. Again, in the words of Charles Bolton, the father-in-law of the protagonist Hans, the readers understand that the current policy of the US government is a faulty one. Charles Bolton states: "I actually believed in deterrence, so I suppose that helped. This lot are a different kettle of fish. One simply doesn't know what they're thinking" (p. 25). Thus, Charles Bolton is contrasting between the Cold War and the War on Terror. During the Cold War, deterrents worked because there were identifiable countries with stated territorial integrity, but in the War on Terror, deterrents do not work because even the players cannot be identified for certain.

In fact, Charles Bolton argues that deterrents will make matters worse. Charles Bolton states: "They're likely to take some encouragement from what happened, don't you think?" (p. 25). Obviously, what the book is meaning is that the War on Terror will only multiply the number of terrorists and terror that could be perpetrated against the United States. In other words, there is direct relationship between War on Terror and the growth of terrorism; greater the war on terrorism, the greater activity of the terrorists. After the response of Charles Bolton, the narrator's comments confirm this direct relationship between the War on Terror and the growth of terrorism. The narrator states: "In short, there was no denying the possibility that another New York calamity lay ahead and that London was probably safer" (p. 25). The book's position is that New York will definitely encounter another major terrorism. Zadie Smith notes: "In the end what is impressive about *Netherland* is how precisely it knows the fears and weaknesses of its readers. What is disappointing is how much it indulges them."[52] Smith is, in essence, successful because it points out the angst of the American people. American people oppose George W. Bush and the War on Terror because they represent further destabilizing element in the world, which could lead America further into insecurity.[53]

---

[52] "Two Paths for the Novel," http://www.nybooks.com/articles/22083
[53] Lustick notes: "The War on Terror is the enemy of the American people, overshadowing threats posed by terrorist" (Lustick, *Trapped in the War on Terror*, p. 115).

Thus, in the book, Rachel takes Jake, the son of Hans and her, to London, away from New York. The novel, *Netherland*, identifies US militarism as a threat to the world and to individual lives in America, by aggravating a revenge-response scenario. Many Americans can identify with this assessment of the current American foreign policy, as characterized by *Netherland*. On top of that, many American citizens are fed up with the costly War on Terror, which they blame in part for the economic troubles in America. It is not surprising, therefore, that the American people decided to vote in those who, they thought, would end the pointless War on Terror.

It cannot be gainsaid that the victory that the Democrats enjoy with dominance in the US Senate, US House of Representatives, and the US Presidency is due to George W. Bush's militarism. Pedersen states: "Public dissatisfaction with the war was cited as one of the main reasons that voters turned to the Democrats and gave them control of both houses of Congress. The war had proved an albatross, not only for George W. Bush, but also for those Democrats who had supported him in 2002.

In the late 2006, Obama's characterization of the war as 'dumb' looked more prescient than misguided."[54] Pedersen describes Obama's victory over Democratic Presidential nominees, Clinton and Edwards, as due in large part to their support of war in Iraq. Pedersen explains:

> In the course of 2007 a number of candidates announced that they were seeking the Democratic nomination. Polls showed that many Americans viewed the War in Iraq as one of the most important issues for the forthcoming election in 2008. Obama used his early opposition to the war to his advantage during the primary campaign. The two other

---

[54] Pedersen, *Obama's America*, p. 153.

frontrunners, Hillary Clinton and John Edwards, were forced to explain why they had voted as they had in 2002. Edwards expressed regret; Clinton never entirely disavowed her decision to support Bush.[55]

Thus, Obama is currently in the White House because he publicly opposed US militarism in Iraq. Even Obama's bitterest opponents understand that Obama centralized his anti-war platform during his presidential campaign. Dick Morris and Eileen McGann state: "Obama camouflaged his domestic agenda behind the single overshadowing position of opposition to the war in Iraq."[56] Although Morris and McGann criticizes Obama's "socialist" domestic policies primarily, the statement is telling in that Morris and McGann implicitly recognize the primary public platform that won Obama victory in the presidential race was the anti-war position. Morris and McGann explain how Obama's public platform of anti-war delivered him the victory: "The swelling casualty count in Iraq disenchanted Americans and distracted them from the importance of preserving our national security. Isolationism and obliviousness to the obvious costs of a premature pullout became the order of the day. As public opinion moved to the left, driven by the incompetence of George W. Bush's war strategy, Obama seemed to offer a reasonable alternative. His antiwar position – once easily dismissed as turning tail – now looked like a rational position."[57] It is not the American people who have changed their opposition to US militarism in the Middle East since the game-changing election; it is Obama.

Joseph O'Neill's book, *Netherland*, is indeed a gauge to measure American sentiment about the War on Terror and their

---

[55] Pedersen, *Obama's America*, p. 153.
[56] Dick Morris and Eileen McGann, *Catastrophe: How Obama, Congress, and the Special Interest Are Transforming … a Slump into a Crash, Freedom into Socialism, and a Disaster into a Catastrophe … and How to Fight Back* (New York: Harper, 2009), p. 7.
[57] Morris and McGann, *Catastrophe*, p. 7.

distrust of politicians, including President Barack Obama, who are bent on continuing this war, which they consider as immoral. Christopher Tayler writes: "O'Neill has said that he wrote the book as 'an American novel ... My first novel as an American novelist', and in this respect, he seems to have succeeded."[58] The pessimism about America's future in regards to the global War on Terror, in which President Barack Obama is currently ensnared, indicates the predicament of America and Americans, led by President Obama. Ian S. Lustick best describes the catch-22 of the global War on Terror:

> America's counterterrorism effort has a life of its own. Americans are not in charge of the War on Terror; the War on Terror is in charge of us. The array of slogans, bureaucracies, lobbying strategies, wars, budgets, contracts, books, television shows, films, cottage industries, and academic centers that makes up the War on Terror has come to operate as a self-organizing, self-perpetuating whirlwind – a veritable hurricane of public policies and private ambitions that feed on one another and on the impossibility of any outcome we could know as "victory." We are disoriented, drowning in red ink, distracted from crucial domestic and foreign policy problems, and led astray into counterproductive disasters, most notably in Iraq.[59]

Now, under President Barack Obama, the disaster that entraps America into a cycle of destruction – economic, social, and

---

[58] "Christopher Tayler finds Joseph O'Neill on a sticky wicket with his novel of New York cricketers, Netherland." *The Guardian.* June 14, 2008
(http://www.guardian.co.uk/books/2008/jun/14/saturdayreviewsfeatures.guardianreview7/print)

[59] Lustick, *Trapped in the War on Terror*, p. 48.

Netherland **by Joseph O'Neill & President Barak Obama's AMERICA**

institutional – is the War in Afghanistan. Joseph O'Neill's novel, *Netherland*, best illustrates this as a way of allegory.

Netherland by Joseph O'Neill & President Barak Obama's AMERICA

"Chuck Ramkissoon and the History and Character of Trinidad"

Chuck Ramkissoon, a Trinidadian of Indian descent, who in essence opens the novel, *Netherland*, and closes it, can be seen as a symbol of the failure of the American dream. The American dream can be identified as economic success and social acceptance. Having been murdered, Chuck Ramkissoon achieved neither. In a sense, Chuck Ramkissoon embodies what is wrong with American capitalism as portrayed by Joseph O'Neill, the author of the novel. To understand the significance of the phenomena, it is important to understand Chuck Ramkissoon as a character, shaped by his ethnic identity and history. The history of Trinidad, in essence, helps to clarify to the reader the gravitas of Chuck Ramkissoon as a character and to explain to an extent the ramification of his symbol as the failure of the American dream.

In essence, 9/11 shows Rachel, the wife of Hans the narrator, how futile her Capitalist pursuits are. Rachel, in fact, packs up her things in New York City, a city which perhaps best embodies American capitalism, and takes her son and returns back to England, the land of her birth. In a sense, therefore, Rachel makes a reverse migration or return-immigration. Her return is a message that America is not the New Land of happiness, but rather a place of disappointment and a mirage that is filled with curses, rather than blessing. Rachel's return is an affirmation that the American Dream is spurious for white collar workers. There is a significant white collar worker migration to the USA for economic gain, and Rachel represents the spurious nature of such a Capitalist pilgrimage.

This disenchantment of Rachel is not isolated; many white collar workers in New York and in other metropolitan areas feel a sense of purposelessness. This is evident in the case of Christopher Gorman who used to make a seven figure salary and seven figure bonuses. One day, Christopher Gorman said to himself, "Why are we living in this huge house with all of this stuff that keeps breaking that we don't even need?"[60] Thus, Christopher Gorman moved to Elbow Cay, part of the Bahamian island of Abaco, with his wife and his three children (newly born, aged 3, and aged 6). Christopher Gorman felt similar sentiment with Rachel's and decided to get out of the rat race of American capitalism. In a sense, the American dream is seen as broken. To achieve serenity and peace, one has to leave. So, Christopher Gorman and Rachel in *Netherland* left. Obviously, not everyone has the economics to leave. And America is a land of immigrants, and not a land of white collar migrants.

Netherland by Joseph O'Neill depicts the American dream of immigrant dreams coming true as corrupted and largely unachievable because of socio-political factors at play. Chuck Ramkissoon embodies an ideal immigrant who is capable of achieving his American dream. Chuck is clever, driven, and hard-working. And Chuck believes in the American dream. Furthermore, Chuck comes from Trinidad, a place which does not offer the possibilities that America does economically. Thus, throughout the book, readers find themselves rooting for Chuck to succeed, although they know the ending from the very beginning of the book. Chuck is killed horrifically.

Although Trinidad is poor, it has a long and interesting history of self-actualization and black empowerment, so it is not surprising that Trinidad has produced a powerful character, like Chuck Ramkissoon, who is a tragic hero that the readers root for, even knowing that he is to die prematurely. Understanding the history of Trinidad helps the readers understand better the tragedy of Chuck Ramkisson's final end.

Trinidad stands in stark contrast to the USA in the popular conception. Trinidad was claimed by Christopher

---

[60] Monte Burke, "Downshift," in *Forbes*, Vol. 185, No. 7 (April 25, 2010, pp. 63-66), p. 63.

Columbus for the Spanish Crown on July 31, 1498, during his third voyage. Christopher Columbus himself named the place Trinidad.

Christopher Columbus remained less than one week in Trinidad, only long enough to establish contact with some native Americans, and then Columbus sailed north to Hispaniola, which was the principal seat of government of the Spanish Empire in the New World. The next twenty-five years were uneventful; Spanish traders occasionally stopped by Trinidad, primarily to seize native Indians for slave labor in the gold mines of Hispaniola and Puerto Rico.

Spain did not begin colonizing Trinidad until about 1530. For many years, a small group of Spanish colonialist lived in Trinidad with weak executive authority, trying to fend off foreign incursions. In 1595, Sir Walter Raleigh came to Trinidad and destroyed the capital founded three years earlier by San José Oruña, the Spanish governor of Trinidad, and Sir Raleigh withdrew from the island shortly afterwards.

For the next century, English, Dutch, and French marauders invaded Trinidad. For the first two hundred years of Spanish colonial rule in Trinidad, colonial governors did not have enough colonialists to form an effective military force, so a kind of mutual self-interest bound the Spanish colonialist and their conquered subjects.

By the end of seventeenth century, Roman Catholicism was firmly entrenched among the native population. In 1687, Royal Cédula ("decree") was issued, granting native Indians who were baptized a status as vassals of the Spanish Crown twenty years after baptism, and thereby they would be freed from slave labor. By 1700, slave labor of native Indians was abolished in the colony.[61]

Until the eighteenth century, Trinidad was not well-developed, because Spanish imperialist policies developed by the Spanish Crown long before prevented European settlement

---

[61] Alvin Magid, *Urban Nationalism: A Study of Political Development in Trinidad* (Gainesville: University of Florida Press, 1988), pp. 22-23.

in the colony and marginalized its international economic potential. Foreign citizens could not settle in Trinidad and could not handle external trade.

Blight struck the plantations around 1725, and economic recovery did not occur until sixty years later. But the situation improved, when in 1776, Spain allowed French citizens who were Roman Catholic to settle in Trinidad. In the next two years, 1,000 French Catholics and their 1,500 slaves entered Trinidad.[62]

On November 24, 1783, the Spanish Crown promulgated a new Cédula ("decree") opening Trinidad to foreign immigration and for developing the colony. This new decree allowed all Roman Catholics, regardless of their country of origin, to come to Trinidad as colonialists, provided that they swear oath of allegiance to the Spanish Crown. After five years, the new Roman Catholic settlers could become citizens of Spain.[63]

Although Protestants were barred from immigration to Trinidad, the last Spanish governor of Trinidad, Don José María Chacón, who was liberal and open-minded, permitted many Protestant settlers – white, black, and mulatto – to enter the colony in the period of 1784 to 1797.[64] These colonialists would get land; white colonialists would get twice as much as free black and mulatto colonialists.[65]

The policy was very liberal for the time since it allowed free blacks to own land and slaves. Thus, slavery in Trinidad was not along the color lines; both whites and free blacks owned slaves from the very beginning of slavery in Trinidad, which began with the new decree of 1783, over seventy years before the American Civil War.

One year after the decree of 1783, the population of Trinidad nearly doubled; in 1784, the population of the colony

---

[62] Magid, *Urban Nationalism*, p. 27.
[63] Magid, *Urban Nationalism*, p. 28.
[64] Magid, *Urban Nationalism*, p. 28.
[65] Magid, *Urban Nationalism*, p. 28.

reached 6,503. In the last year of Spanish rule in 1797, the colony had 17,718 inhabitants. And the number of free blacks increased as well. The number of free black colonialists in 1797 was 4,476. And the number of black slaves in 1797 was 10,009. However, the native Indian population decreased to 1,082 in 1797 from 2,200 in 1782.[66] Three centuries of Spanish rule drove the native Indians to virtual extinction.

Trinidad entered the next phase of its history, when Great Britain acquired Trinidad from Spain in 1797, and secured its claim to the island in 1802, under the Treaty of Amiens. In 1802, 48.3% of the 2,261 whites in Trinidad were French citizens. And 63.7% of the free population of Port-of-Spain was French. In contrast, 88.1% of St. Joseph was Spanish.[67] The French in Trinidad were known for cultivating cocoa.[68]

Although the British were the minority in Trinidad, British colonialists immediately began to agitate for English civil law and a constitution modeled after those of other British colonies. However, Britain feared that such reforms would disrupt the peace, given the large French and Spanish population, and rejected the proposals. Instead, the Parliament established a Crown Colony government in Trinidad that would report directly to London.[69]

In 1834, slavery system was abolished in Trinidad, and an apprenticeship system was implemented, which ended in 1838, two years before its expected completion.[70] In 1838, there were 22,359 emancipated slaves.[71] The apprentice system was to acclimate the emancipated slaves to their new status of freedom and to encourage former slave owners to adapt to the new system.

---

[66] Magid, *Urban Nationalism*, pp. 28-29.
[67] Magid, *Urban Nationalism*, p. 29.
[68] Magid, *Urban Nationalism*, p. 30.
[69] Magid, *Urban Nationalism*, p. 39.
[70] Donald Wood, *Trinidad in Transition: The Years after Slavery* (London: Oxford University Press, 1968), p. 10.
[71] Wood, *Trinidad in Transition*, p. 39.

The premature ending of the apprentice system created suspicion in the minds of freed slaves that the old system was lingering on. Donald Wood states: "The old cries of neo-slavery are reminiscent of the modern cries of neo-colonialism."[72] This claim is apt because the dominant minority in Trinidad was Anglicans and the majority of the Christians were Roman Catholics, thereby creating a situation similar to Ireland. Wood states: "In this respect Trinidad is more like Ireland in the same years than like Jamaica or British Guiana."[73] The history of Trinidad explains why Joseph O'Neill, an Irishman, used a Trinidadian as his protagonist.

It is because Trinidad's black population received emancipation before their counterparts in the South of the United States that one finds fugitive American slaves in Trinidad in the nineteenth century. Escaped American slaves who had fought in the Corps of Colonial Marines against their former masters in the War of 1812 were disbanded in the Bahamas, and some of them were sent to Trinidad. In 1815 and succeeding years, they settled in seven villages named after their companies in the Savanna Grande region. Sergeants and corporals were entrusted with the responsibility of keeping peace in these villages. Liberated African slave women were sent to the villages to be wives for the retired soldiers.

By 1824, there were 923 in these settlements, and they were referred to as "Americans" by the Trinidadians. They were seen to be hard workers, and often left their villages to work elsewhere. By 1838, there were 828 residents in these settlements. Since these "Americans" were from the South, they were highly emotional Baptists who maintained their brand of Christian religiosity.[74]

In Joseh O'Neill's literary work, *Netherland*, Chuck Ramkissoon's wife represents influence from this strand of Trinidadian history. In fact, Chuck Ramkissoon's mother took

---

[72] Wood, *Trinidad in Transition*, p. 10.
[73] Wood, *Trinidad in Transition*, p. 10.
[74] Wood, *Trinidad in Transition*, p. 38.

part in Baptist religious ceremonies after Chuck's brother's death. In *Netherland*, Chuck describes Trinidad's Baptist movement while recounting the fight between his father and mother,

> The fight was because my mother wanted to take part in a Baptist ceremony for my brother. You know who the Baptists are? …. The Baptist Church is this Trinidad brew of Christian and African traditions – you'll see them in Brooklyn on a Sunday, wearing white and ringing bells and trumpeting the spirit. They believe spirits take possession of you. Sometimes one of them will catch the power on the street, shaking and trembling and falling to the ground and speaking in tongues. It's a spectacle. The other thing people associate with Baptists is sacrificing chickens (p. 242).

Since Chuck Ramkissoon is Indian, his father did not subscribe to Christianity. Chuck's mother dabbling with the Baptist church angered Chuck's father, who thought of Christianity as a black people's religion. Chuck's father cut off a chicken's head and threw it at Chuck's mother in anger. Chuck describes, "So you can see why my father did what he did. He was angry my mother was falling for this black people's voodoo" (p. 242). It is ironic that Chuck Ramkissoon married such a Baptist and became a Baptist like his mother; this can be seen as his rebelling against his father and his Hinduism sensibilities, and siding with his mother and identifying with her pain at his brother's death. Chuck Ramkisson's description of Baptists of Trinidad jives in large extent with the historical reality of the Baptist movement in Trinidad. Wood describes the religiosity of the South which impacted Trinidad as the result of the settlements by emancipated American slaves:

Their services were apocalyptic and noisy, and caused concern to the staid English Baptist ministers who visited them. In the tradition of the Deep South, their great festival was the camp meeting which sometimes lasted a week. Their thunderous preaching and singing was sometimes discussed in the newspapers; in the mid-nineteenth century it was considered less of a threat to the dissemination of more orthodox religion than the introduction of heathen immigrants. Two streams of religious experience met in their worship, a West African one of rhythm and the dance, and the Puritanism of sixteenth-century Münster and East Anglia; their fusion brought about "shouting" and jumping and shaking by those who felt themselves the chosen of the Lord of Hosts. They started a fashion in the religious life of Trinidad that has persisted, in spite of official disapproval, until the present day.[75]

This is this brand of religiosity that Chuck Ramkissoon's wife embraces in *Netherland*.

Although emancipation brought active religious participation by former black slaves and had other positive elements, there were some negative outcomes as well.

In Trinidad, one of the major problems of emancipation was squatting. Emancipated slaves did not want to live in the plantations where they worked. Thus, villages spontaneously appeared along the roads as freed slaves set up tent. Many emancipated slaves set up their residence in other people's property or government property. Government was ineffective in driving out the squatters. Vast amount of lands in Trinidad was ignored. Wood describes: "But it was far easier to squat on both private and Crown lands. In August 1838, it was

---

[75] Wood, *Trinidad in Transition*, pp. 38-39.

estimated that of the 208,379 acres in private ownership only 43,265 acres were in cultivation and there were in addition over 1 million acres of Crown land."[76] Often, squatting occurred in lands that were not monitored well. But the lack of anti-squatting laws often made guarding private property against squatters ineffective.

Laws were passed to solve the squatting problem. The Proclamation of March 30, 1839 (giving effect to an Order in Council of October 6, 1838) authorized Stipendiary Magistrates to evict squatters of less than one year and to imprison them for up to 6 months, if they did not leave within fourteen days after their conviction.[77]

However, planters themselves refused to inform on the squatters because they provided needed labor for their plantations. Thus, anti-squatting laws had little effect. Wood describes: "Lewis Pantin, the proprietor of Bon Aventure near Pointe-à-Pierre, declared that he would never denounce a settlement of fifty to sixty squatters in his neighborhood; he needed their labour and, if they were moved, another planter elsewhere would benefit."[78]

Perhaps, the concept of living on the edge or even breaking the law in the open is inherited by Chuck Ramkissoon, a Trinidadian in New York City who engages in illegal activity as if it were acceptable, in *Netherland*. Just as legality was subsumed under market necessity in Trinidad's history, Chuck Ramkissoon believed that the principle applied in the USA. In a sense, Chuck Ramkissoon applied Trinidadian worldview in the American scene. The laborers in Trinidad could develop a swagger because they were needed and essential for the economy of Trinidad, and the plantation owners recognized this. Thus, Trinidadian laborers received higher wages than those in other islands. For example, at Emancipation,

---

[76] Wood, *Trinidad in Transition*, p. 49.
[77] Wood, *Trinidad in Transition*, p. 51.
[78] Wood, *Trinidad in Transition*, p. 51.

Trinidadian laborer received 20 cents a task, whereas a laborer in Barbados received about 20 cents per day.

The labor pay continued to rise in Trinidad, so by June, 1840, the pay reached 50 cents per task and in some plantations 60-65 cents for fieldwork.[79] This represents 250% to 325% increase in pay in two years. Furthermore, many plantations provided free houses and free provisions of salted fish and rum to all those who worked for them.[80] This kind of demand certainly must have created a strong sense of self-worth among Trinidadians, which *Netherland*'s Chuck Ramkissoon exhibits. Wood describes the auspicious condition of Trinidad's laborers:

> Frederick Maxwell, the manager of Philippine Estate, who had himself been a slave before he was liberated for good conduct by his owner, allowed his mill and boiling-house people one cooked meal, two or three glasses of rum, and half a pound of salted cod daily. For a task the average allowance seems to have been one glass of rum and half a pound of salt fish.[81]

Frederick Maxell illustrates another important point. Due to economic necessity, former black slaves were used as managers with authority and given great latitude. This explains the managerial and entrepreneurial spirit that Chuck Ramkissoon exhibits in *Netherland*; he was, in effect, a product of such a history of the colored people in Trinidad.

Another important point to note is that Anti-Slavery Society in England was carefully monitoring what was going on in Trinidad and protested any actions that resembled slavery. Naturally, freed laborers being drunk on the provided rum and becoming alcoholics were of concern to the Anti-Slavery Society in England, which saw rum as a type of control mechanism to

---

[79] Wood, *Trinidad in Transition*, p. 53.
[80] Wood, *Trinidad in Transition*, p. 53.
[81] Wood, *Trinidad in Transition*, p. 53.

subjugate the black population. Thus, on January 1, 1842, free allowances of rum were stopped, as churchmen looked happily on.

Still, labor conditions in Trinidad continued to the advantage of the laborers, and this spelled difficulties for the employers. Wood describes: "They wanted a regular and docile force with a low turnover but instead they had mobile labourers who would not be bound by any contract and who would leave to seek better conditions if they pleased."[82] In a sense, therefore, Trinidad's labor force was mobile and self-negotiating from the beginning, which explains Chuck Ramkissoon's mobile, entrepreneurial activities, at least in part.

Despite the inducements for Trinidad's freed slaves, many of them did not return to plantation work. Thus, there was drain of workers continuing. Trinidad's plantation owners first sought blacks from nearby Caribbean islands, America, and Africa. By the end of 1850, 3,157 Africans from Sierra Leone and 2,676 Africans from St. Helena had gone to Trinidad.[83] From Africa, the British home government only accepted immigrants from Sierra Leone and St. Helena.[84] By 1861, immigration from Africa ended with total from Sierra Leone being 3,383 and from St. Helena being 3,198.[85]

However, it was the Indians from Asia who ultimately provided the solution for Trinidad's labor problems.[86] Indians were preferred to the Chinese for plantation labor, and Chinese laborers were procured mostly by British Guiana, which was in a worse condition than Trinidad.

Only about 2,500 Chinese ever went to Trinidad, mostly in the seasons of 1853, 1862, 1865, and 1866, and they are the ancestors of the Chinese population of 4,700 in Trinidad some hundred years later.[87]

---

[82] Wood, *Trinidad in Transition*, p. 54.
[83] Wood, *Trinidad in Transition*, p. 79.
[84] Wood, *Trinidad in Transition*, p. 77.
[85] Wood, *Trinidad in Transition*, p. 80.
[86] Wood, *Trinidad in Transition*, p. 60.
[87] Wood, *Trinidad in Transition*, p. 160.

The first shipload of Chinese for Trinidad was recruited in December 1805 by a Portuguese trader, who gathered 141 Chinese men in Macao and ferried them to Penang in Malaysia. This Portuguese trader was paid 25 Spanish dollars for each one. The Portuguese trader recruited another six Chinese men in Penang. Together, 147 Chinese men had two captains, Affat and Awar, and they went to Trinidad via Bengal. They were to be a part of the experiment in social engineering for the New World. Each Chinese man received $6 per month and the two captains, Affat and Awar, received $15. If they wanted, they could return to China at no cost.[88] It is evident that this social experiment was to become the model for later Indian migrant worker arrangement, although later Indian laborers were given preference to Chinese laborers in Trinidad.

In total 194 Chinese men were brought to Trinidad to comprise "the first settlement of Chinese outside Asia."[89] This included 53 Chinese men who were recruited in Calcutta, India, to add to the 147 Chinese men from Penang, Malaysia, who had arrived in Calcutta to board the *Fortitude* in May, 1805, bound for Trinidad; six Chinese immigrants died on the voyage.[90] In a sense, therefore, the first settlement of the Chinese in Trinidad is significant to the history of Chinese immigration and indeed to the history of Chinese people as a whole.

The social engineering experiment in Trinidad using the Chinese was the result, in part, of the proposal by Captain William Layman of the British Royal Navy, who had seen how Chinese labor had transformed Penang, Malaysia. Captain Layman said that the Chinese were "inured to a hot climate, and habitually industrious, sober, peaceable, and frugal, and eminently skilled in the culture and preparation of every article of tropical produce."[91] Captain Layman argued that slave labor

---

[88] Kim Johnson, *Descendants of the Dragon: The Chinese in Trinidad 1806-2006* (Kingston: Ian Randle Publishers, 2006), p. 16.
[89] Johnson, *Descendants of the Dragon*, p. 16.
[90] Johnson, *Descendants of the Dragon*, p. 20.
[91] Johnson, *Descendants of the Dragon*, p. 17.

is less efficient than using Chinese free labor; he said that a 640-acre sugar plantation in Trinidad would cost £49,690 to establish using 250 black slaves, in contrast to £26,435 with 100 free Chinese laborers.[92] Not only would sugar plantation owners save money, but they would have less workers to worry about and manage.

Furthermore, Captain Layman stated that since Chinese free laborers were civilized free men, they would provide an example to the blacks and help avert rebellion.[93] Captain Layman further argued that as the number of Chinese middle class increased, they would serve as a buffer between the whites and the blacks.[94]

But Captain Layman was troubled by one fact; the Chinese seemed to have no problem of cohabitation with people of color and the Chinese did not mind the child of the union submitting to "the conditions of the mother."[95] In other words, one reservation that Captain Layman had was that the Chinese would begin to intermarry with local blacks in Trinidad and raise their children to benefit the black mother and her racial group. However, despite some reservation Captain Layman encouraged using Chinese migrant workers.

Based on the recommendation of Captain Layman, the Colonial Office of the British Empire sought the advice of George Staunton, who had recently returned from Canton, where he had served the East India Company. Although Staunton thought that it would be difficult to contract agricultural laborers, especially since emigration was considered a treasonable offence punishable by beheading, Staunton said that Chinese were adaptable and familiar with the cultivation of sugar cane, which was the primary industry in Trinidad.

Thus, the Colonial Office of the British Empire accepted the recommendation from Captain Layman seeking 2,000

---

[92] Johnson, *Descendants of the Dragon*, p. 17.
[93] Johnson, *Descendants of the Dragon*, p. 17.
[94] Johnson, *Descendants of the Dragon*, p. 18.
[95] Johnson, *Descendants of the Dragon*, p. 18.

migrants to be recruited at Penang, Malaysia, but the social experiment was to be highly secretive, and the plan was to be kept strictly confidential from the British Admiralty, the East Asia India Company, the French, and the Dutch. In 1803, Kenneth MacQueen, a private contractor familiar with the Chinese, was to set up a post in Penang, which was to be kept a secret from the Chinese and Batavian governments, for the purpose of recruiting Chinese men.[96] MacQueen was, therefore, instrumental in collecting 194 Chinese men for Trinidad's social engineering experiment; the *Fortitude* arrived on October 12, 1806.[97]

The social engineering experiment with the Chinese migrants failed within a couple of years. Within one year after their arrival of 194 Chinese men, 61 Chinese men returned with the *Fortitude* in July, 1807. By October, one year after their arrival when the government stopped their stipend, 17 Chinese men died in Trinidad. In the second year, most Chinese men were trying to return by whatever means possible.

By 1809, fewer than 30 Chinese men were left in Trinidad. The census of 1810 described "a colony of 22 Chinese males who lived in misery in Cocorite, making their living selling charcoal, oysters and crabs."[98] The failed Chinese experiment brought the scorn of the English. James Stephen said that "a negro did as much in a week as one of them in a month."[99] Even John Black, who was selected to look after Chinese interests in Trinidad, suggested that the Chinese men be sent back home.[100]

But Kim Johnson argues that it was the socio-economic environment that sealed the failure of the Chinese experiment: "But most people agreed the Chinese men were industrious and blamed their unproductivity on a lack of agricultural experience.

---

[96] Johnson, *Descendants of the Dragon*, p. 19.
[97] Johnson, *Descendants of the Dragon*, p. 20.
[98] Johnson, *Descendants of the Dragon*, p. 20.
[99] Johnson, *Descendants of the Dragon*, p. 20.
[100] Johnson, *Descendants of the Dragon*, p. 20.

These explanations ignored the awfulness of the slave condition and obvious fact that the Chinese would not want to enter the lowest occupations which were badly paid, despised...."[101] Certainly, socio-economic factors played a role in the failure of the social engineering experiment in Trinidad. And waves of Chinese immigration and migrant workers failed to take hold in Trinidad.

In 1824, there were only about a dozen Chinese left in Trinidad, and in 1834, according to E. L. Joseph, there were only seven Chinese left in Trinidad.[102] The Chinese experiment of the first half of the 1800 was a complete failure.

One reason for an unsuccessful wave of Chinese migrants is due to the fact that the Philippines and Indonesia were close to China, and it was not easy to persuade the Chinese to sail half a way around the world for labor.[103]

Furthermore, a later impetus for Chinese migration to Trinidad was due largely due to the cessation of Indian migration in 1849, when the planters urged the colonial government to import them, again, out of lack of choice. In 1851, the Legislative Council passed a resolution to bring 1,000 Chinese coolie laborers to Trinidad with a 5-year contract with no free return passage.[104] The Colonial government of Trinidad had learned from their experience in the first decade of 1800 that given the opportunity for free return, Chinese migrants would return. In this, the Chinese were, in fact, worse treated than Indian laborers in the mid-1800s because Indian laborers were given free passage back.

From 1853 to 1854, eight ships (*Australia, Clarendon, Lady Flora Hastings, Maggie Miller/Wanata, Montrose, Paria, Dudbrook, Red Riding Hood*) brought 2,645 Chinese to Trinidad; there were 309 female Chinese.[105] But the Chinese had a high

---

[101] Johnson, *Descendants of the Dragon*, pp. 20-21.
[102] Johnson, *Descendants of the Dragon*, p. 22.
[103] Wood, *Trinidad in Transition*, p. 160.
[104] Wood, *Trinidad in Transition*, p. 161.
[105] Johnson, *Descendants of the Dragon*, p. 28.

mortality rate in Trinidad. About 20% of those who landed with the ship *Australia* in 1853 were dead within one year, generally from ulcer and fever.[106]

But despite the difficulties, the Chinese in Trinidad came to prosper through a combination of saving, trade and successful gambling. The game of "Whe-Whe" was brought to Trinidad by the Chinese in 1853, and is their cultural contribution to Trinidad, which lasts to this day, despite the official disapproval.[107] The Chinese were so good at business that by 1857, there were reports that the Chinese were driving out Indian and Portuguese retailers out of business.[108]

Furthermore, many Chinese decided to settle down in Trinidad and become assimilated. In 1857, five Chinese married Creoles, and another three Chinese planned to marry Portuguese-speaking black women from the Cape Verde Islands.[109] Other intermarriages with locals followed. The Chinese were prone to integration. Kim Johnson states: "Certainly, it is true that the Chinese were less bound by cultural prejudices and more inclined than Indians to adapt to their environment."[110] Fifteen Chinese in Trinidad converted to Catholicism in 1857 and two to Anglicanism.[111]

Despite minor successes of Chinese immigration, especially in terms of numbers, Indians were eventually to dominate not only Trinidad's immigration scene, but also the economic and political realms, as the most powerful minority group.

In *Netherland*, Chuck Ramkissoon, who was of Indian descent, represents the descendants of the new migration of workers from India to Trinidad who eventually became a very strong voice in Trinidad's politics and society.

---

[106] Wood, *Trinidad in Transition*, p. 163.
[107] Wood, *Trinidad in Transition*, p. 163.
[108] Wood, *Trinidad in Transition*, p. 163.
[109] Wood, *Trinidad in Transition*, p. 163.
[110] Johnson, *Descendants of the Dragon*, p. 31.
[111] Wood, *Trinidad in Transition*, p. 163.

Indians were not always welcome to Trinidad, however. In fact, in 1840, emigration of Indian laborers, derisively called "coolies", was stopped by Parliament after protests by both Houses. The Anti-Slavery Society opposed Indian immigration into West Indies because of what they perceived as a type of slavery being reinstituted there after alleged ill-treatment in Mauritius, where Indians have been arriving since 1834, and in British Guiana, where four planters had brought in about four hundred Indians as a private venture in 1838.

When there was a campaign to compel the British Imperial Government to readmit Indians into Mauritius and West Indies, Trinidad was noticeably absent in the push. Wood states: "India was considered the country of last resort, the *ultima Thule* of immigration."[112] In 1843, immigration of Indians to Mauritius was reopened with the stipulation of official supervision, to which the Court of Directors of the East India Company did not object. On July 13, 1844, Stanley wrote to the Governors of British Guiana, Trinidad, and Jamaica that immigration of Indians to West Indies was allowed. Trinidad received 1,000 Indians and other two colonies 2,000 each in the first season.[113] And this set into motion a complete ethnic remaking of the Caribbean with great influx of Indian immigrants for decades. Wood states: "No one foresaw that by this permission, so significant in the history of the West Indies, a movement of people was being set in train that was to go on with only minor interruptions until 1917, and that the whole balance of ethnic forces in British Guiana and Trinidad was to be radically altered by the Indians who chose to settle in the Caribbean."[114] In 1851, 173 Indians from Calcutta, India, landed in Trinidad, and the Indian immigration as indentured servants continued until 1917, when indentured Indian immigration ended in the British Empire.[115]

---

[112] Wood, *Trinidad in Transition*, p. 107.
[113] Wood, *Trinidad in Transition*, p. 109.
[114] Wood, *Trinidad in Transition*, p. 108.
[115] Wood, *Trinidad in Transition*, p. 130.

Chuck Ramkissoon's ancestry and heritage go back to this period in Indian history. The majority of the Indians were from Calcutta, and Tamil and Telugu speakers accounted for only 10%.[116] Thus, it was northern Indians who set the tone for the Indian community in Trinidad. Wood describes: "For the 1867-8 and 1868-9, 46.5 per cent (2,977) of the 6,384 men, women, and children registered for Trinidad came from the North-West Provinces, 27.9 per cent (1,786) from Oudh, 16.2 per cent (1,037) from Bihar, and only 5.4 per cent (346) from all Bengal. The remaining 4 per cent were from central India (36), the Punjab (27), Orissa (22), the native states (11) and from 'miscellaneous places' including Bombay and Madras (196)."[117]

And the Indian migration to Trinidad was not merely from the low classes. The Brahmin upper class Indians often comprised a major segment of the Indian migrants. For example, in the 1868-9 season, the Brahmin class comprised the second largest group among the *Poonah*'s passengers and in the 1880-1 season, the third largest group among the *Jumna* passengers. Often, the Brahmin had to falsify their caste status in order to migrate to Trinidad because English officials believed that the Brahmin made bad workers and would not allow some of them to migrate to Trinidad for labor purposes.[118] Thus, it must be assumed that more than the official number of the Brahmin class migrated to Trinidad. Wood presents official statistics of migration:

> But between 1876 and 1885, when annual records were being kept in Calcutta, 21,288 emigrants were registered for Trinidad of whom 17,741 were Hindus, 3,535 were Muslims, and twelve were Christians. Of the Hindus 18 per cent were Brahmins and other high castes, 32 per cent were from agricultural castes, 8.5 per

---

[116] Wood, *Trinidad in Transition*, p. 143.
[117] Wood, *Trinidad in Transition*, p. 145.
[118] Wood, *Trinidad in Transition*, p. 143.

> cent were from artisan castes, and 41.5 per cent were recorded as low-caste. No significant changes in the recruitment areas took place in the 1870s nor did the kinds of people who emigrated alter. One can assume that a similar balance between the four caste groups held broadly true in the 1850s and 1860s.[119]

Thus, it is clear that a significant part (18%) were Brahmin, or upperclass of India. For Indians, Trinidad provided economic opportunity, and even upperclass Indians were willing to indenture themselves for a chance at economic prosperity.

There were two types of indentured servanthood for Indians in Trinidad. Indians who came before 1854 were generally granted free passage back to India after 5 years of indentured servanthood. Those Indians who arrived in Trinidad after January 1, 1854, were bound to ten years of indentured servanthood before being given assistance to travel back to India. Both groups required indentured servanthood initially of three years, and then they were given choices. They could reindenture themselves with an employer of their choice to finish out their industrial residence in Trinidad or they could pay £6 lump sum or 5s per monthly tax until their industrial residence was completed.[120] In this sense, the Indians in Trinidad were singled out from other laborers. Wood states: "In this way the Indians were subjected to a restraint on their freedom or to a tax that did not affect the rest of the population."[121] However, it was possible for Indians to take up trade or business that they were familiar with in India after their indentured servitude was over, whereas many of the indigenous colored people had to continue working in the field for their economic survival. Wood describes: "Many [Indians] took this opportunity; by the end of 1855 there were about 2,000 Indians

---

[119] Wood, *Trinidad in Transition*, p. 145.
[120] Wood, *Trinidad in Transition*, p. 135.
[121] Wood, *Trinidad in Transition*, p. 135.

with certificates of industrial residence, but only 509 were on yearly contracts."[122] Thus, it can be said that Indians were a type of colored merchant class in Trinidad.

In *Netherland*, Chuck Ramkissoon embodies the entrepreneurial spirit that characterized indentured Indian servants in Trinidad, and thus Chuck Ramkissoon can be seen as a type of indentured Indians in Trinidad's history, who work hard to eventually rise to the middle class or higher in the society.

Ironically, however, Indians of Trinidad were often socially subjugated under the black indigenous population of Trinidad who had won emancipation from slavery. A part of the reason for this was that the indigenous black population had gone into power structures of Trinidad society, whereas Indians remained purely in the business realm. Wood describes Indians' inferior position in Trinidad:

> By these measures the indentured labourer was set apart from the rest of the population. He alone carried a pass book and he alone was an object of suspicion if he were seen idle on the roads and villages. It was easy for him to become the butt of an officious police constable who perhaps wanted to show off in front of a crowd of Creols. "Slave, where is your free paper?" was reported to be the taunt of Negroes toward Indians as late as 1873, when many of the immigrants had become respectable ratepayers.[123]

Such taunting of Indians by blacks in Trinidad did not occur only in the nineteenth century; in fact, such racial taunting could be found in the twentieth century, as experienced by Dr. Rudranath Capildeo, a Bramhim with roots in city of Gorakhpr

---

[122] Wood, *Trinidad in Transition*, p. 135.
[123] Wood, *Trinidad in Transition*, p. 136.

not far from Napal, who eventually became one of the important leaders of the Democratic Labour Party in Trinidad. Oxaal describes the racial taunting that Capildeo received from blacks in the prestigious Queen's Royal College in Port of Spain, Trinidad:

> There were few other Indian boys at Q.R.C. during the early Thirties. Out of 366 scholars enrolled during one year, 60 were of European descent, 6 were Indians, while the majority of the remainder were Negroes, largely sons of civil servants and professional families. Although his closest friend was a Negro, young Rudranath's experiences with many of the Creoles were highly traumatic. To them he was the little Coolie boy from Chaguanas. Some Negro classmates, exercising what they implicitly believed was the Creole birthright, taunted and bullied him. He was continually involved in fights. Once, when he was a few years older, he knocked down an antagonistic fellow member of the Cadet Corps, and would have killed him with the butt of a carbine, but was restrained before he could land the blow. His humiliation as a "Coolie boy" was not limited to the sadism of his classmates, however, for even his teachers made occasional sport of his backwardness.[124]

As Oxaal's description shows, in Trinidad, blacks felt a sense of superiority over Indians even in the twentieth century. Thus, it is not surprising that Chuck Ramkissoon, who was of Indian descent, married a black Trinidadian, named Anne; it was, in a

---

[124] Ivar Oxaal, *Black Intellectuals Come to Power: The Rise of Creole Nationalism in Trinidad & Tobago* (Cambridge: Schenkman Publishing Company, Inc., 1968), p. 162.

sense, upper social mobility. To illustrate this point, Joseph O'Neill uses the color language. Joseph O'Neill writes in *Netherland*: "Anne Ramkissoon ... was an African Caribbean woman of around fifty, markedly paler than Chuck, with very short hair" (page 157). The fact that the Indian Chuck was darker than the African Anne was a way of showing the pecking order of Indians vis-à-vis Africans in the Trinidadian social context. Joseph O'Neill was, in essence, utilizing the color politics of the USA, where fairer skinned African-Americans are often described as being of higher status than darker skinned African-Americans. Even in terms of social respectability, the African Carribean Anne was a church-going woman, who was preparing chicken for her senior pastor's birthday, whereas Chuck Ramkissoon was dealing in shady business along with some legitimate ones. This description fits the social stratification that divided African Caribbeans and Indians in Trinidad; Indians were seen as inferior to African Caribbeans in Trinidad.

However, Indians have steady grown in size. According to 1960 census, Indians (Hindu and Muslim) comprised about 36.5% of the population, which was 827,957, to 43.5% blacks; in contrast, Europeans comprised 2% and the Chinese 1%.[125] A part of the reason why blacks remained the majority in Trinidad is due to the fact that the British government preferred to maintain a black majority among the minority groups.

Although Indian migration was encouraged, the British government preferred to have internal Caribbean movement and encouraged movement between the islands, rather than migrants from India or China. Wood notes: "From the end of 1839 to the end of 1849, 10,278 West Indians were said to have gone to Trinidad; during the same period 7,582 went to British

---

[125] Selwyn D. Ryan, *Race and Nationalism in Trinidad and Tobago: A Study of Decolonization in a Multiracial Society* (Toronto: University of Toronto Press, 1972), p. 3.

Guiana but only 790 to Jamaica."[126] But there were not that many people in the Caribbean to recruit workers from.

During the similar period, beginning with July 1839, when William Burnley as Trinidad's agent tried to recruit America's black freedmen to Trinidad, far smaller number immigrated from America. Wood states: "By June 1847, 1,301 Americans mainly from Delaware, Maryland, New Jersey, Pennsylvania, and New York had come to try their luck in the colony."[127] From the vantage point of the US government, emigration of black Americans, as long as they were not runaway slaves, was okay. Although Americans had arrived with much fanfare to Trinidad, most of them left because America' blacks tended to be craftsmen and mechanics, whose labor was more suited to urban areas, rather than the plantation settings of Trinidad. In 1848, only 148 Americans remained in Trinidad.[128]

The situation was obviously different for Indians; they were suited to rural environments of Trinidad. Increased migration and social and economic mobility created deep shifts in Trinidad's social and political environment. All of it came to a head in the 1880s, which saw unprecedented unrest and revolt.

1880s was a period of deep transitions; there were revolts by all three racial groups. The revolt of the blacks of Trinity occurred in 1881 in the Carnival Riots, the revolt of the Indians occurred in 1884 in the Hosay riots of 1884, and the revolt of the whites occurred in 1887 in the Reform movement.[129]

The native-born population of Trinidad was 82,500 in 1881, and 12,000 were born in Trinidad of Indian parents. Total population in Trinidad in 1881 was 153,128, and 46% of them, or 70,000, were born outside of Trinidad. The largest number of

---

[126] Wood, *Trinidad in Transition*, p. 66.
[127] Wood, *Trinidad in Transition*, p. 67.
[128] Wood, *Trinidad in Transition*, p. 68.
[129] Anthony de Verteuil, *The Years of Revolt: Trinidad 1881-1888* (Port-of-Spain: Pariah Publishing Co., Ltd., 1984), p. xi.

immigrants was from India, numbering around 45,000.[130] In Trinidad in 1881, out of 153,128 residents of Trinidad, about 100,000 were classified as "creoles,"[131] or blacks. This group was heterogeneous socially; there were black middle class, the black rural masses, and black urban laborers. Even in terms of language, there was diversity among black creoles: French, Spanish, and English. There was difference also in terms of religious affiliation; some blacks were Roman Catholic and others were Anglican and non-conformist. But all blacks showed a growing pride in their race in the 1880s.[132] Father Massé describes the growing black pride of the 1880s: "The most ragged negro wants to be called Mister."[133]

However, blacks were divided into different classes. There were wealthy blacks and poor blacks; there were educated blacks and uneducated blacks. There were black civil servants, and there were black day laborers and black factory workers. One thing all these blacks shared was the Carnival.

The Carnival came from France to Trinidad when French settlers and heir slaves came to Trinidad after the Cedula of 1783. At first, the Carnival was celebrated primarily by rich colonialists in masked balls, but eventually free blacks began to celebrate the Carnival in their own way. In 1830s, the Carnival came to be accepted as the celebration of the whole community. The fact that the communal celebration of the

---

[130] De Verteuil, *The Years of Revolt*, p. 13.

[131] Bridget Brereton states: "'Creole' is a word which has accumulated many meanings. In the later nineteenth century, it meant a person born in Trinidad of European and/or African descent. This would be the most usual interpretation when the word was used without any qualifying adjective. A 'white Creole' was a person born in the island of European descent; a 'Creole Indian' was born in Trinidad of East Indian descent; a 'Creole Spaniard' was an individual of Spanish (and often African and Amerindian) descent born in the island" (Bridget Brereton, *Race Relations in Colonial Trinidad 1870-1900* <Cambridge: Cambridge University Press, 1979>, pp. 2-3).

[132] De Verteuil, *The Years of Revolt*, p. 44.

[133] De Verteuil, *The Years of Revolt*, p. 45.

Carnival that had mixed racial presence is attested in the 1831 diary entry of Frederich Urich, a merchant's clerk:

> Sunday 13th Feb. After dinner we went to see the negroes dance. Monday 14th Feb. I went to call on the Bocks but he told us that she was getting ready to attend the disguised ball. Entrance fee $8.00. We follow various masked bands. The dances are usually African dances, and the enthusiasm of the negroes and negresses amuse us very much, for these dances are stupendous. We play smart and look on at the ball for a short time from the street, and then return home and go to bed.[134]

After the emancipation, the Carnival became much more boisterous as all freed slaves participated in the Carnival celebrations in the streets. Even as late as 1886, the tradition of the Carnival was maintained, and upper class Spaniards would wear costumes and visit their friends and watch from their balconies the boisterous black revelers in the streets.[135] In the history of the Carnival in Trinidad, 1868 marked the primary shift, however. Until that time, the Carnival was mostly innocent fun, with masquerades of pirates, soldiers, red Indians, etc.

However, in 1868, urban lower class, called "Jamet," came to give the Carnival their own stamp, and the Carnival came to be known as "The Jamet Carnival." The Jamet Carnival encouraged involvement of the criminal elements and prostitutes, and the Carnival began to develop a strong sexual element with explicit sexual horseplay, such as men wearing transparent clothing acting like women with menstrual-blood covered cloth visibly displayed, gyrating their hips in sexual motion. In the streets, lewd, explicitly sexual songs were sung,

---

[134] De Verteuil, *The Years of Revolt*, p. 57.
[135] De Verteuil, *The Years of Revolt*, p. 58.

and the women were directly propositioned for sex.[136] A notable feature of the Jamet Carnival was the Canboulay, which involved a procession of masked men, carrying lighted torches, and the Canboulay started on Sunday (Dimanche Gras) night and continued until Monday morning.[137] In 1880s, Canboulay was celebrated in many towns and villages, although Port of Spain was the main center.[138]

Although legislation had been introduced in 1868 to control the Carnival, making the carrying of lighted torches an offense when done to the harm or danger of any resident or passenger in the street, the law was not strictly enforced until Captain Baker became Inspector Commandant in 1877.

The Carnivals of 1878 and 1879 were strictly controlled and stick-fighting, which had been an important part of the Jamet Carnival, became essentially prohibited. In 1880, Inspector Commandant Baker used the 1968 Ordinance to suppress the Canboulay, and he called on the participants to surrender their torches, sticks, and drums. The crowd complied, and the newspapers responded by supporting Inspector Commandant Baker's actions. *Port-of-Spain Gazette* reported on March 1, 1879:

> It may fairly be claimed as one of the happy results of Captain Baker's short administration of the Police Force, that fighting in the Streets on a large and dangerous scale during the Masquerade time has been rendered almost impossible. This hearty reaction has been brought about by the departure from the insane policy of former years, of turning out whole detachments of Police to witness as passive spectators the affrays and riots which we were told it was impossible to put down. ....

---

[136] De Verteuil, *The Years of Revolt*, p. 60.
[137] De Verteuil, *The Years of Revolt*, p. 62.
[138] De Verteuil, *The Years of Revolt*, p. 63.

> Captain Baker, with the assistance of a couple of mounted Officers of Police, has managed to impress upon the savage and ferocious hordes which would have swallowed up the whole Police Force of former times, that there is now a living authority to enforce a strict observance of the Peace on these two days.[139]

Another praise of Inspector Commandant Baker comes from *New Era* on February 16, 1880:

> Thanks to the activity and firmness displayed by the Police under the direction of Capt. Baker, the Carnival this year was a marked improvement over the orgies of the late past. What order and decorum were really possible under the characteristic of a saturnalia, having so large an element of not as the Cannaille as a necessary component, Capt. Baker maintained, at the expense of much personal exertion, attended, we are quite sure, with much inconvenience to himself, to say nothing of the risk incurred.[140]

However, the risk manifested itself in 1881, when great hostilities between the people and the police broke out. The problem, of course, was that blacks felt that the Carnival was an important part of their tradition. Even upper middle class blacks felt solidarity with lower middle class blacks on the cultural value of the Carnival.[141]

1882 and 1883 Carnivals were filled with unrest and violence. The clash of 1882 between the black revelers and the police was inevitable. In anticipation of the violent conflict, the

---

[139] De Verteuil, *The Years of Revolt*, p. 68.
[140] De Verteuil, *The Years of Revolt*, p. 70.
[141] De Verteuil, *The Years of Revolt*, p. 73.

Government sawmills produced over 140 new baton sticks capable of cracking a person's head open with one blow. In response, the mob armed themselves before the Carnival with sticks, stones, and bottles. The harbinger of the conflict came in the form of an anonymous placards posted throughout the town on Friday or Saturday before the Carnival, which stated: "News to the Trinidadians: Captain Baker demanded from our just and noble Governor, Sir Sanford Freeling, his authority to prevent the rite of Can Boulay, but Our Excellency refused."[142] The placards were meant to encourage civil resistance and to show the police as illegitimate. By Sunday night, all over the city, black masses knew that resistance to the police was planned.

At 11:30 PM, 150 police officers were paraded by Captain Baker, who was determined to stop the carrying of the torches. When the clock struck midnight, the Nègres-Jardins who had been waiting for one hour in the Eastern section of the town struck their drums, sounded their horns, lit their torches, and broke out into Kalinda songs. A very large Nègres-Jardin band came up St. Vincent Street, turned east up Park Street towards Dry River. Captain Baker was waiting, mounted on his horse, and he ordered his policemen to seize the torches. The police rushed the crowd, but the crowd did not disband. Fighting ensued that lasted two hours. Although the police won in the end of the struggle, 38 out of 150 police officers at the scene were injured, which necessitated recruiting new police officers for the next day, which was the second day of the Carnival of 1882. The Government Notice read: "A serious and disgraceful disturbance having occurred last night in the Town of Port of Spain, and in view of a possible renewal of the same, all well-disposed persons are invited to attend at the Police Barracks in Port of Spain to be sworn in as Special Constables. The Stipendiary Justice will attend at the Court for this purpose today and on such other days as may be found necessary."[143] In

---

[142] De Verteuil, *The Years of Revolt*, p. 76.
[143] De Verteuil, *The Years of Revolt*, p. 86.

a sense, a type of state of emergency existed as the result of the clash between the police and the black residents of Port-of-Spain. The situation was so bad that the Governor delivered a speech to quell the black masses. Governor Freeling delivered a speech to the black mob in the Eastern Market at 5 PM:

> My Friends, I have come down this afternoon to have a little talk with you. (Cheers). I wish to tell you that it is entirely a misconception on your part, to think that there is any desire on the part of the Government to stop your amusement. (Cheers). I know everybody at times likes to amuse himself – I have no objection to amuse myself whenever I have an opportunity. I had no idea what your masquerade was like. If I had known, you should have had no cause for dissatisfaction. There has been entirely a misconception on all sides, for the only interference was the fear of fire – I thought that the carrying of torches ... at this time might be attended with danger, and I was anxious to guard against it. That was the only objection: it was the fear of fire and nothing more.[144]

Obviously, the Governor's speech was an effort at appeasing the angry mob. A midnight, the black crowd came by the hundreds to the Police Station and jeered at the police. At the Governor's orders, Captain Bakers told the police to stand down. The crowd outside held a mock funeral of Captain Baker and burned him in effigy.[145] The mocking of the police by the crowd had the result of 58 police officers resigning on the Carnival Tuesday, less than a day after the Governor's speech

---

[144] De Verteuil, *The Years of Revolt*, p. 91.
[145] De Verteuil, *The Years of Revolt*, p. 93.

and the crowd taunting the police.[146] De Verteuil describes the effect of the Carnival clashes of 1882: "When the police returned to duty they were often jeered at and pelted with stones, and for some time had to patrol parts of the town in pairs. Undoubtedly, the authority of the police had been undermined and the worst elements of society became very truculent."[147] Captain Baker, in response, sent a letter dated March 9, 1881, to the Secretary of State for the Colonies, which read:

> Sir, I most respectfully beg on behalf of the Force I have the honour to command that His Excellency the Governor may see fit to appoint a commission to inquire into the circumstances and origin of the late disturbances and of the attack upon the police on the morning of the 26th ultimo and the 1st instant. My non-commissioned officers and men are daily subjected to the pelting of stones and to the jeers and insults of the lower public and false reports are circulated as to my personal behavior during the late disturbance of which I have had no opportunity of refuting. My wife and children are even insulted whenever they show their faces in the streets. I have etc. A. W. Baker, Captain.[148]

In response, ironically, the Colonial Office officials blamed the Governor and Captain Baker, rather than the black masses which revolted. Sir R. Herbert, the Permanent Under-Secretary, stated: "It is tragic that their officials should be so ignorant as not to know that the Carnival nuisance has to be suffered at Rome, Nice, Paris etc. etc. notwithstanding some incidental

---

[146] De Verteuil, *The Years of Revolt*, p. 94.
[147] De Verteuil, *The Years of Revolt*, p. 95.
[148] De Verteuil, *The Years of Revolt*, pp. 95-96.

danger and much annoyance to sober citizens – and that the police might as well try to prohibit Londoners from going to the Derby. They must be reprimanded when we hear the full reports."[149] Since the Colonial Office considered the Governor of Trinidad and the police captain at fault, the black masses won a concrete and historically significant victory against the colonialist power structure. Although Trinidad's black population did not fully comprehend the extent of their victory, they knew that they had beaten the police and the government. This victory can be seen as marking the inevitable black power movement that became political and eventually wrested power away from the dominant whites in Trinidad.

Indian empowerment took a different route, as Indians and blacks of Trinidad were distinct groups who vied for economic advantage and political power. Indians worked primarily in Trinidad's sugar industry as laborers. Unfortunately for the Indians of Trinidad, the sugar industry of Trinidad took a hit in 1884, when Germans dramatically increased beet production. And France doubled its government subsidy and increased sugar production in France, so cheap beet sugar flooded the British market, which was the traditional market for West Indian sugar. Deflation of Trinidad's sugar prices ensued. In 1884, 60,961 tons of sugar were exported and were worth only £642,255. However, just a year before, in 1883, 54,496 tons of sugar, which represents the total export of sugar from Trinidad in 1883, were worth £886,172.[150]

The great deflation in the value of sugar within one year is clearly visible, and this caused problems for Trinidad's sugar industry. The problem for the sugar plantation owners was that despite their great loss of profit, they could not reduce the wages of their sugar plantation laborers. By law, indentured laborer's wages could not be reduced. And when sugar plantation owners tried to lower the wages of non-indentured laborers, they threatened to leave. Since their labor was

---

[149] De Verteuil, *The Years of Revolt*, p. 96.
[150] De Verteuil, *The Years of Revolt*, p. 125.

essential to the sugar industry in Trinidad, sugar plantation owners immediately rescinded reduction in wages for non-indentured laborers. What the sugar plantation owners did to get around this problem was to force indentured laborers to work harder than before.[151] Although the wages of indentured laborers, who were mostly Indian, could not be reduced, Indian laborers often opted for pay per task, rather than wage pay. Previously, Indian indentured laborers were able to perform up to three tasks per day. But with the sugar price deflation of 1884, Trinidad's sugar plantation owners increased the difficulty of each task, so that an Indian indentured laborer could not do three tasks like before. Thus, the pay per Indian laborers decreased since many of them were paid per task. Thus, the annual remittance per Indian to India dropped to £4-4-2 in 1884 from £4-10-11 in 1883.[152]

What contributed to united Indian uprising in 1884 was the fact that Hindu Indians and Muslim Indians came to share a common holiday and festival celebration in Trinidad. The Hosay Festival of the Shia Muslim sect was first celebrated in Trinidad in 1850 on the Philippine estate south of San Fernando, and it quickly spread to other estates. In 1863, the Hosay Festival was officially recognized by the government as Queen Victory granted permission for Hosay Festival to be observed in Trinidad as long as there were Indian residents. After Queen Victoria's blessing, this Hosay Festival came to be celebrated by Indian Hindus and Muslims, alike. By 1880, the Hosay Festival came to be a unified "national" festival for Trinidad's Indians, and Indians used the Hosay Festival to demonstrate their power.[153] De Verteuil comments: "But whatever the reason, the Hosay by 1880, had acquired a sort of symbolic value in the eyes of the Indians. Their cultural life, their national life, their self-esteem

---

[151] De Verteuil, *The Years of Revolt*, p. 126.
[152] De Verteuil, *The Years of Revolt*, p. 126.
[153] De Verteuil, *The Years of Revolt*, p. 136.

were concentrated in the celebration of this Hosay or Mohurrum Festival as it was officially known...."[154]

The Hosay Festival is celebrated on the 10th day of Muharram (or Mohurrum), the first month of the Islamic Calendar, in order to coincide with date Imam Hussain, the grandson of the Prophet Mohammed, was slaughterd in Kerbala, Iraq. The Hosay Festival was introduced by Shia Muslims, a minority Muslim sect. Shia Muslims were among the Indians brought to Trinidad to be indentured laborers. Since Indians who adopted the Muslim faith in India did not completely abandon their Indian and Hindu roots, there are common forms of celebration that both Hindus and Indian Muslims could enjoy. The Sunni Muslims, which is the majority Muslims, observes Hosay with additional prayers, fasting, reading the Koran, and distributing alms to the poor. But it is not the Sunni Muslim's austere observance of Hosay which dominates Indians of Trinidad, but rather the festive Shia Muslim version.[155] Shia Muslim's focus on the celebration of the "martyr's moral victory."[156]

Interestingly enough, the most disorderly Hosay celebration occurred in the same year as the Carnival riots of 1881. Several months after the Carnival riots, a leading Indian Harracksingh, a Christian Indian, was killed by Filipinos, as Harracksingh tried to win the right for his estate to lead the San Fernando procession.[157] The disturbance raised the alarm of the white colonialists, since they had seen public discussion about the Indian threat to Trinidad, especially in the 1870s. The *New Era* stated on April 3, 1871: "The day is not far off when these Coolies, bent on having everything their own way, and meeting with the slightest resistance on the part of the authorities, will break out in open rebellion, and reproduce here the barbarities of the great chief Nana Sahib in British India a

---

[154] De Verteuil, *The Years of Revolt*, pp. 137-138.
[155] De Verteuil, *The Years of Revolt*, p. 138.
[156] De Verteuil, *The Years of Revolt*, p. 139.
[157] De Verteuil, *The Years of Revolt*, p. 143.

few years ago."[158] And fear of Indian uprising grew even more as the Indian population in Trinidad exploded from 1871 to 1881. In 1871, there were 27,425 Indians (25% of Trinidad's total population) in Trinidad, but in 1881, there were 48,820 Indians (31.8% of Trinidad's total population) in Trinidad. So, many non-Indians came to be reminded of the potential Indian threat during the Hosay Festival. De Verteuil comments: "Prejudice against the Indians fed more and more on fear – and fear of them particularly at Hosay time."[159]

Haplessly for the Indian community in Trinidad, there were some Indian Muslims who protested the Hosay Festival. Early in 1882, a few Indian Muslims went to the Rev. K. J. Grant, a Canadian Missionary among the Indians, and asked for his advice regarding their protest against Tadjahs, which they considered idolatrous. Rev. Grant suggested that they petition the Governor. Soon, 107 Indian Muslims signed a petition and placed it in the hands of Governor Sanford Freeling. The Indian Muslim petition stated:

> We are the Mussulmans of Trinidad. We believe in one God. We abhor all idol worship. This Taziyadari is one form of idol worship and is no part of our religion. When people drink rum and like vain fellows swing their sticks and shout Hasan and Husain before Taziya we get much shame because gentlemen think that this is the Mahommedan religion. Neither in the Koran nor in any Sacred Book of ours are we told to make Taziya. In this play quarrels arise, injuries are inflicted, bones are broken, men are killed, and it is our good name that gets reproach, hence we are in distress. Our religion rose in Arabia, and we have amongst us many Arab people all faithful Mussulmans and none

---

[158] De Verteuil, *The Years of Revolt*, pp. 143-144.
[159] De Verteuil, *The Years of Revolt*, p. 145.

of them ever heard of Taziya. On account of our distress we entreat your Excellency to issue an order for the discontinuance of this play, and whilst we live we will remember your kindness, and praise your name for having judged so wisely.[160]

Emboldened by this, Governor Freeling drew up an Ordinance regulating the Festivals of Immigrants in July, 1882, and the Ordinance was sent to the Secretary of State for the Colonies in London for approval. The Immigrants Festivals Ordinance 1882 empowered the Governor to make regulations regarding the routes of festivals and to maintain people.[161]

On July 30, 1884, Regulations were promulgated that targeted Hosay celebration as traditionally practiced. The Regulations called for strict control with up to six headmen to control the festival processions. Also, non-Indians could not participate in the Hosay Festival. And the headmen had to be Muslims. Furthermore, the Regulations stated: "No such processions will be allowed to enter the precincts of the towns of Port of Spain or San Fernando, nor will any such processions be allowed to use or cross any high road or public road except on the express permission in writing of the stipendiary magistrate of the district in which the procession shall pass."[162] The Regulations were meant to hinder any involvement of black Trinidadians in the Hosay Festival, for fear that the two minority groups might be unified in protest against the British colonial government.

Furthermore, the Regulations were intentionally meant to disenfranchise the Indian Hindu population, which was the dominant population among Indians of Trinidad.[163] In response, Sookoo, the headman of the Philippine estate which generally

---

[160] De Verteuil, *The Years of Revolt*, p. 146.
[161] De Verteuil, *The Years of Revolt*, p. 148.
[162] De Verteuil, *The Years of Revolt*, p. 158.
[163] De Verteuil, *The Years of Revolt*, p. 160.

led the San Fernando Hosay procession, who was a Hindu, sent a petition, signed by headmen of various estates on September 22, 1884, which stated: "That your petitioners view with sorrow and alarm the intention of the Government under which they serve to suppress their annual festival of Hosein, which your petitioners have hitherto always celebrated with the strictest regard to decorum as becoming their religious obligations."[164] Obviously, many Indians considered the Ordinance and the Regulations as an effort to suppress the Indians in Trinidad. Such perception ironically galvanized the Indian masses of Trinidad.

Although Trinidad's colonial government was reacting against the disturbances of the Carnival riots and perceived itself to be trying to preserve the peace, their actions further confirmed in the minds of Indians in Trinidad of their own need for political empowerment and political participation. Colonial Secretary's reply was read at the San Fernando Police Court directly to Sookoo and fifteen other petitioners in order to ensure avoidance of riots like those pertaining to the Carnival. The colonial government reply stated: "The Regulations do not in any way interfere with the religious rites connected with the festival, nor indeed have the Government the slightest desire to infringe those rites, but no procession can possibly on the ground of religion claim to enter the towns of Port of Spain or San Fernando, or to proceed along the high roads of the Colony without the permission of the magistrate of the district."[165] Obviously, this was a political way of prohibiting the procession and giving the runaround. Religious processions have been historically important for Christianity as well, as Via Delarosa shows. Clearly, Trinidad's colonial government was intending to control the subjugated population and break the morale of the Indian population. But their plans backfired, and the colonial prohibitions galvanized the Indian masses into a purposeful political entity.

---

[164] De Verteuil, *The Years of Revolt*, p. 161.
[165] De Verteuil, *The Years of Revolt*, p. 163.

Personally, Sookoo responded to the colonial response with rage. Sookoo said, "Mutiny, there will be a Mutiny. If there is evil, let evil come!"[166] Sookoo's vow for revolt came at a bad time for Trinidad's colonial government. In 1884, there was a drastic fall in sugar prices, and there had been twelve labor strikes, the largest number of any one year from 1870 to 1900.[167] Non-Indians of Trinidad feared Indians and wanted to suppress them, and their sentiments carried publicly. Regarding the Indians of Trinidad, *Port of Spain Gazette* stated in October 18, 1884: "They are united while we are divided. …. Let the coolies know that they will, in all cases, be severely punished, whenever they attempt to take the law in their own hands. [The Government] must devise means to break down the power of the Brahmins."[168]

The October 1884 uprising of the Indians of Surinam, in essence, showed the non-Indians of Trinidad that their fears were justified. The uprising in Surinam resulted in soldiers killing seven Indians and arresting the ringleader. At the same time, there was an uprising in the El Socorro estate, near Port of Spain, in which Indian indentured laborers resorted to violence, complaining that the tasks given them were too difficult. The police were prevented by Indian masses from arresting the ringleaders after Indian indentured laborers attacked the overseer of El Socorro estate, and the solders had to be brought in to make the arrests. In response, the colonial government of Trinidad sent circulars to some 83 estates throughout Trinidad, announcing the regulations. Estate managers were told to post the regulations for Indian indentured laborers to see. Answer to Sookoo's petition was sent to some 26 estates, so that it could be read to Sookoo (again) and other petitioners, who resided there. The Indian response was silence, and that

---

[166] De Verteuil, *The Years of Revolt*, p. 164.
[167] De Verteuil, *The Years of Revolt*, p. 164.
[168] De Verteuil, *The Years of Revolt*, pp. 165-166.

troubled the colonial government since Hosay was to take place on October 30th.[169]

By October 28th, there was wide perception that trouble was in the air. Captain Baker stated: "After that (the night of the 27th) information reached me from all quarters that the coolies were determined to come into San Fernando on the Thursday. I did not think myself they would make the attempt but nevertheless did not lessen precaution to prevent them."[170] However, Captain Baker proved to be wrong; Indians united to rebel against the proclamation of the colonial government. Indians were going to have their Hosay procession in San Fernando, come what may. De Verteuil describes: "As was the case with at Carnival when the bands united to fight the police, so here at Hosay they were to unite to force their way into San Fernando."[171] Thus, 1880s could be seen as a period of group solidarity, that of the black Trinidadians on the one hand and that of Indians on the other hand, and the historical process was largely facilitated by bungling efforts of the colonial government of Trinidad.

On October 30th, non-Indian shopkeepers closed their shops after rumors of disturbance spread, and Indian shopkeepers also closed their shops, but with the intent of participating in the Hosay processions with their fellow Indians.[172] At 1:30 PM, reports arrived that thousands of Indians were approaching San Fernando in processions from all directions: 2,500 from the Northern districts, 4,000-5,000 from the South, and 1,900 from Guaracara and the East.[173] The conflict resulted in gunfire by the police and death of 12 Indians and about 100 Indians injured, according to John Scott Bushe, the Administrator.[174] *New Era* reported on November 3rd: "The news of the slaughter of the coolies have (*sic*) caused a certain

---

[169] De Verteuil, *The Years of Revolt*, pp. 166-167.
[170] De Verteuil, *The Years of Revolt*, p. 173.
[171] De Verteuil, *The Years of Revolt*, p. 177.
[172] De Verteuil, *The Years of Revolt*, p. 178.
[173] De Verteuil, *The Years of Revolt*, p. 182.
[174] De Verteuil, *The Years of Revolt*, p. 193.

sensation in Port of Spain where public opinion does not approve of the policy: the Government are deemed to have acted with haste and undue severity."[175]

In response, the Secretary of State for the Colonies telegraphed Sir H. W. Norman, the Governor of Jamaica, to make an official inquiry. Norman arrived in Trinidad via Barbados on December 31st. After one week of investigations, Norman concluded that Indian revolt was not tied to economic grievance, but rather to their intransigence in "the notion that they are powerful and could do what they please. .... They should be firmly but kindly dealt with."[176] De Verteuil feels that such a judgment was biased and comments: "One cannot help but feel that the conclusions of the commissioner were not completely free from bias, and that his stay of one short week was not altogether adequate for an analysis of the situation."[177] There were not any real disturbances by the Indians after 1884. Ironically, Indians turned to acquisition of personal wealth and participation in the system to gain power, rather than taking the road of revolt. This was to lead to the political empowerment of the Indians decades later to the scale unimaginable in the 1880s.

The unrest of the 1880s was not confined to the blacks and the Indians, even whites contributed to the unrest of the period. A part of the reason for this was that the white society was very hierarchical in nature and such a rigidity did not fit the fluidity of the colonial existence. De Verteuil describes:

> Victorian Trinidad was a rigidly structured society, as we have seen, and no sector was more hierarchical than the white. The Portuguese, for example, were classified almost automatically as lower class, along with the few 'poor whites' (generally of Irish descent) who

---

[175] De Verteuil, *The Years of Revolt*, p. 193.
[176] De Verteuil, *The Years of Revolt*, pp. 194-195.
[177] De Verteuil, *The Years of Revolt*, p. 195.

had emigrated from other West Indian islands. The middle class, overseers, shop assistants, clerks, non-commissioned officers in the police, were mainly English or Scottish expatriates with a few creoles, and could move up to the upper class by marriage or acquisition of wealth. The upper class, which some writers refer to as 'the white élite', (though probably this term would not have been recognized or acknowledged at that time), dominated social, economic and political life in Trinidad. It consisted of two main groups. First, the British officials in the most important posts and with them the wealthy English creoles, that is, Trinidadians born of English parents or Englishmen who had made Trinidad their home and who were creoles by adoption. The second group were the French creoles. More numerous than the English, they were mainly whites of French descent; but the term was generally understood to include people of Spanish, Irish, Corsican and German descent, and almost invariably Roman Catholics. As was the case with the English creoles, people born in Europe and habituated by a long residence to the French creole society were considered creoles.[178]

Because social elitism was tied to government and political rule,[179] it is not surprising that white ethnic groups and white

---

[178] De Verteuil, *The Years of Revolt*, pp. 202-203.

[179] It is important still to note that most British officials in Trinidad were career colonial officials who stayed in Trinidad until promoted elsewhere; salaries in the West Indies were lower than those of India, the Far East, or even Africa, which were considered more prestigious and glamorous (Brereton, *Race Relations in Colonial Trinidad 1870-1900*, p. 56).

individuals who were not in the political leadership structures would be prone to revolt.

Trinidad had a colonial structure under British imperial rule, and so the colonial government of Trinidad had a fundamental interest in keeping the colony running smoothly at the colony. The British Crown was interested in maintaining Trinidad's sugar interests and sugar plantations. Thus, the Legislative Council in Trinidad basically protected British interest and the British governor in Trinidad, and ensured British dominance among the ruling class. De Verteuil states: "Apart from controlling the Legislative Council, the British sugar interests also exercised influence on the Colonial Office through the West India Committee in London which more and more came to represent only the British Guiana and Trinidad sugar companies."[180] Thus, it is not surprising that the British Crown appointed "unofficials" to be a part of the Legislative Council, and these unofficials were drawn from sugar plantation owners primarily. Between 1862 and 1898, unofficial held a majority in the Legislative Council. But these unofficial actually worked to prop up the power of the British Crown. It is not surprising in light of the stated purpose of unofficial of the Legislative Council, which the Duke of Buckingham, the Secretary of State for the Colonies, enumerated in a circular dispatch in 1868. The Duke of Buckingham stated that the unofficial member of the Legislative Council "will naturally understand that holding his seat by nomination of the Crown, he has been selected for it in the expectation and in the confidence that he will co-operate with the Crown in its general policy, and not oppose the Crown on any important question...."[181] In a sense, the unofficial of the Legislative Council was an insurance policy to maintain British imperial interests in Trinidad.

Many whites who were not British or were not interested primarily in protecting British interests instigated a revolt of sorts in the form of "the Reform movement" in order

---

[180] De Verteuil, *The Years of Revolt*, p. 211.
[181] De Verteuil, *The Years of Revolt*, pp. 209-210.

to change the constitution to give more power to non-British whites.[182] In the Legislative Council, there were French creoles and Catholics, non-British individuals, but they had little influence since the majority was controlled by the British unofficial who represented sugar interests, and they were dominant in the 1870s and into the 1880s.[183] Since the British sugar interest dominated Trinidad in the late 1800s, those who were tied to British sugar interests were opposed to the Reform movement. De Verteuil states: "No one who was English oriented, *and* a sugar planter, *and* an Anglican remained for very long in the Reform movement of the 1880's and 1890's; such men, to a large extent, already had control of the Government in their grasp; and so it is those who belonged to any other category, which did not embrace all three requisites above, who formed the heterogeneous reform movement."[184] Even though in historical hindsight, the British control was clearly dominant in the 1870s, economically, socially, and politically, those living at the time did not think this way. For example, in 1882, a top British official stated: "We must destroy the French influence at any price."[185] Some British actually felt that the French interest was a threat to a British-centric Trinidad. The sugar crisis of 1884 seemed to confirm in the minds of many British that their position in Trinidad was precarious. From 1884 to 1885, imports fell by 11% and exports from £1,831,903 to £1,512,314.[186]

Another reason why the British came to fear the Reform movement is that there was a rise in Trinidadian nationalism, particularly among those of French descent. Unlike the British who were able to return to Britain fairly easily, the case was different for the French. Because of the French Revolution and the bad conditions in France in 1830s, those of French descent

---

[182] De Verteuil, *The Years of Revolt*, p. 207.
[183] De Verteuil, *The Years of Revolt*, p. 210.
[184] De Verteuil, *The Years of Revolt*, p. 211.
[185] De Verteuil, *The Years of Revolt*, p. 214.
[186] De Verteuil, *The Years of Revolt*, p. 214.

in Trinidad, or "French creoles," could not easily return to France, so many of the French creoles came to call Trinidad their "home" by the 1880s, unlike the English.[187] Governor Gordon (1866-1870) made some concessions to provide greater equity for French creoles and French Catholics, and there was increased social interaction between the English and the French. Louis de Verteuil called for complete equity in his book, *Trinidad*, published in 1884:

> In a colony like Trinidad where diversity of races will probably continue to exist for many years – a contingency which some may deplore, but which should not disturb their equanimity. In fact, it would be a most suicidal policy on the part of the Government to allow, much less to encourage, any one class of colonists to arrogate to itself a superiority over the rest. More difference of origin, or religion, or of social habits, should not be permitted to raise barriers between different sections of the community; still less should they form an excuse for hedging in a few as a superior estate. Let us toil together in peace, and side by side; it will be for the advantage of all.[188]

Such utopian idealism proved to be the undoing of British rule in Trinidad. In fact, as Trinidad's later history shows, such homogenized society was impossible. Eventually, the blacks drove the whites out of power and completely disenfranchised the Indian minority in Trinidad. Ironically, it was the Reform movement that actually brought about the suicide of British rule and even white rule in Trinidad (including the French creole), and it was the Reform movement that allowed the black power movement in Trinidad to completely disenfranchise minority

---

[187] De Verteuil, *The Years of Revolt*, p. 215.
[188] De Verteuil, *The Years of Revolt*, p. 216.

groups. But historically, a homogenization of the different white groups would necessarily end in the eventual dominance of the blacks in Trinidad, since emancipated black slaves identified themselves with the ethnic origin (French, English, Spanish) of their former slave masters. Louis de Verteuil describes:

> The emancipated class and their descendants bear the distinctive characteristics of their European nations with which they were intimately connected; and these characteristics are to a certain extent borne out by external appearance and deportment of the three specimens: the French negro resembling in these respects a French European, the Spanish a Spaniard and the English negro an Englishman.[189]

While the British dominance held in tact, the white hierarchical structure held both other white groups and former black slaves who identified themselves with their former white slave owners in a form of social and political control. But when the barriers among white ethnic groups fell apart, the whole society was thrown into the mercy of the black majority who ironically became united under the social homogenization of the Reform movement across cultural and social lines. In a sense, Trinidad proves that racial identity is unbreakable, even when political, social, economic, and religious identities are artificially broken.

The Reform impetus came from Philip Rostant, a member of a well-known French creole family, who had developed a sort of "anti-colonialism" and the newspapers. Philip Rostant was an editorial writer for *Port of Spain Gazette* from January 1881 to October 1884. By August 1882, four major newspapers advocated constitutional reform. The Reform movement gained traction due to failed public water

---

[189] De Verteuil, *The Years of Revolt*, p. 218.

works project completed in 1881, which Governor Robinson described as "a lamentable failure."[190]

Furthermore, the "Florence Affair" in Jamaica in 1882, added fuel to the Reform spark. In January, 1882, two official members of the Legislative Council resigned when Lord Kimberly, the Secretary of State for the Colonies, instructed Governor Musgrove of Jamaica to apply to the Legislative Council to cover the cost of lawsuit against Governor Musgrove for his having detained the schooner Florence, carrying ammunition and weapons to St. Thomas, when it arrived in Jamaica with distress on July 22, 1877. Governor Musgrove had been given wrong counsel by his Attorney General and had detained Florence based on that information.

Jamaican newspapers argued that colonial funds should not be financed to pay for the mistakes of officers representing the British Crown, since colonies had no say on the appointment of Governors. The Legislative Council passed a resolution with seven votes of unofficials and five votes of officials against payment. Later, six unofficals would resign. Lord Derby, the new Secretary of State for the Colonies was in favor of a constitutional change, and the Jamaicans agitated for constitutional reform. On March 9, 1883, Prime Minister Gladstone spoke in a way to allow constitutional reform in Jamaica, which in fact was given in 1884.[191] So, the mere sum of £6,700 contributed directly to the eventual loss of power by the British Empire in the Caribbean.

The push for Constitutional reform in Trinidad was compelled by two major factors. In 1884, the British Empire granted Jamaica a new Constitution, setting up a Legislative Council with a Governor, four ex-officio members, two nominated officials, and nine elected members. Six of the elected members could veto a financial proposal unless the Governor declared it to be of chief importance to for the public good. This constitutional reform certainly gave more access to

---

[190] De Verteuil, *The Years of Revolt*, p. 224.
[191] De Verteuil, *The Years of Revolt*, pp. 224-225.

power to those who were not tied to British colonial rule and British interests. Besides the new Constitution in Jamaica, the sugar industry problem of 1884 contributed to the revitalization of the Reform movement.

In 1884, influx of sugar from Germany created a financial crisis in Trinidad, which relied on sugar exports for its economy. The reformers took the opportunity to make demands on the British Empire. On June 4, 1884, Dr. de Verteuil put forward a proposal, which was seconded by Dr. de Boissiere, which implied that Britain hindered Trinidad's competitiveness. The proposal stated: "We claim as an act of justice that the conditions under which we compete with foreign sugar should be more equal and more just."[192] Since the British Empire had control over Trinidad's foreign trade, this statement must be seen as an accusation against the British Empire.

Furthermore, the proposal also sought greater independence for Trinidad in managing its own affairs. The proposal stated: "That the Imperial Government should allow the Government of this island to make reciprocal Tariff arrangements with the United States of America whereby a market for our principal production might be found."[193] This proposal represented a request for more authority to bypass the British Government in London. Thus, the reformists in Trinidad seized the sugar crisis of 1884 to gain dominance over formerly dominant British interests, represented by sugar plantation owners.

And the Reform movement went on the attack. On December 3, 1884, Dr. de Boissiere introduced a motion to reduce the Governor's salary to £4,000, and the motion was seconded by Dr. de Verteuil, his tag-team partner. The vote was taken; however, since the vote was equal, the motion was declared to be lost.[194] Still, it is important to note that the

---

[192] De Verteuil, *The Years of Revolt*, p. 232.
[193] De Verteuil, *The Years of Revolt*, p. 232.
[194] De Verteuil, *The Years of Revolt*, p. 233.

Reform movement was on the attack of the British interest and its titular head in Trinidad, the Governor. This represents a clear galvanization of the Reform movement against the British Empire.

But it was Philip Rostant and his editorials which propelled the Reform movement forward; thus, Philip Rostant was soon the leader of the Reform movement. Philip Rostant was educated in Ireland and lived for years in Ireland. And Philip Rostant owned a cocoa estate in Trinidad and later married an Indian woman from Asia.[195]

Bridget Brereton describes the cocoa industry in Trinidad: "Cocoa was the backbone of French Creole prosperity. The 1860s and 1970s saw their economic recovery; the 1880s and 1890s were decades of relative affluence for the 'third generation' of French Creoles. Prices were consistently high between 1870s and 1918, about £2 18s. 4d. per fanega (110 lb.)."[196] It was this cocoa farmer Philip Rostant who brought some 69 Burgesses to sign a petition for the Mayor of Port of Spain on December 10, 1886, requesting reform to the Constitution. The petition read:

> To His Worship Francis Damian Esq. Mayor of Port of Spain. Sir, We, the undersigned Burgesses of Port of Spain have the honour to request, that, in view of the general wish which now prevails for a moderate change in the constitution of the Legislative Council of the Colony, Your Worship will be pleased to convene a public meeting of the inhabitants of the colony to pass resolutions and take the necessary steps for petitioning Her Most Gracious Majesty on the subject.[197]

---

[195] De Verteuil, *The Years of Revolt*, p. 235.
[196] Brereton, *Race Relations in Colonial Trinidad 1870-1900*, p. 50.
[197] De Verteuil, *The Years of Revolt*, p. 252.

The Reform Meeting was held on January 15, 1887, at 2 PM, at the Savannah just north of Port of Spain. Rostant thought that 15,000 people were present at the meeting to support the Reform. The meeting made Philip Rostant as secretary and Mayor of Port of Spain as the chair.[198]

Members of the Petition Committee were chosen at the meeting, and they met again on January 25 at the Town Hall to formulate the final petition. Philip Rostant did most of the work to draft the petition. The petition cites the example of Jamaica to call for a new Constitution. The petition starts in this way: "We venture to approach the throne, trusting that Your Majesty will graciously deign to listen to our petition which respectfully showeth: 1. That the system of Government which now obtains in this Colony is no longer adapted to the requirements and aspirations of its inhabitants."[199] This was a revolutionary step in light of the history of Trinidad, and it can be seen as a type of white revolt against the British Empire. The Governor Robinson forwarded the Petition to the Queen, and received this reply from Knutsford, the Secretary of State for the Colonies: "H. M. Government are not indisposed to consider whether the colony may not now receive a Constitution as nearly resembling that of Jamaica as the circumstances of Trinidad may justify."[200] Clearly, the Reform movement experienced a victory.

Rostant celebrated after Governor Robinson's public announcement of the news by the Secretary of State for the Colonies on September 24, 1887: "It is with the greatest joy, and may we add, no small degree of self-congratulation that we have to announce to our friends the complete success of the Great Reform Petition."[201] However, the celebration seemed to have been short-lived. On September 30, 1887, Rostant writes: "A paper states that many gentlemen who had signed the Petition have since changed their minds. We do not believe this

---

[198] De Verteuil, *The Years of Revolt*, p. 260.
[199] De Verteuil, *The Years of Revolt*, p. 262.
[200] De Verteuil, *The Years of Revolt*, p. 265.
[201] De Verteuil, *The Years of Revolt*, p. 265.

is possible."[202] Apparently, the 1887 sugar crop was the largest ever, and it is this new crop success which propelled sugar barons to cease their support of the Petition for Reform, which had been propelled largely by the sugar disaster of 1884. Governor Robinson told the Legislative Council on October 27, 1887: "The sugar crop of last season (January) was the largest ever reaped exceeding 87,000 hogsheads."[203]

Still, on January 1888, Governor Robinson appointed members of the Franchise Commission; however, unlike the Jamaican counterpart, Trinidad's Commission included British government officials. But Rostant approved the Council, anyway. The first meeting of the Franchise Commission was held in the Council Hall at Government House on February 2, 1888 at 11 AM.[204] However, the Reform movement failed. Louis de Verteuil states: "The dissenting members were government officials and could not have the same concern in the welfare of Trinidad as its native inhabitants."[205] Unlike Jamaica, Trinidad was not to have elected officials for several more decades. De Verteuil argues that the Reform movement failed most likely due to the objection of the Colonial Office: "Reform failed in 1888 as it was to fail again in 1895 because the Colonial Office (the Secretary of State) was opposed to it. It was only in 1924 that Trinidad was to have its first elected members."[206] Even though the Reform movement in 1880s was a failure, it laid the ground work for fundamental changes to Trinidad in the following decades, which eventually resulted in black empowerment and end to colonialism.

The first general election was held in Trinidad on February 7, 1925, ninety-four years after the British had occupied the island. Out of the registered voters, who numbered 21,794, only about 29% (or 6,832 voters) voted.[207]

---

[202] De Verteuil, *The Years of Revolt*, p. 266.
[203] De Verteuil, *The Years of Revolt*, p. 266.
[204] De Verteuil, *The Years of Revolt*, p. 271.
[205] De Verteuil, *The Years of Revolt*, p. 276.
[206] De Verteuil, *The Years of Revolt*, p. 280.
[207] Ryan, *Race and Nationalism in Trinidad and Tobago*, p. 34.

The TWA President, Captain Cipriani, won 57% of the votes in Port of Spain. Captain Andrew Cipriani was a white French Creole of Corsican descent and had been assigned to the Middle East as a high command of the West India Regiment when the British Empire went to war in 1914. West Indian soldiers fought with British troops and against foreign troops, and Captain Andrew Cipriani felt that they were second to none.[208] This explains how Cipriani came to advocate West Indianization and believed that West Indians could manage their own affairs and did not need British tutelage. Cipriani said that West Indians "were the equals of any Englishman."[209] The white community considered Cipriani as a Bolshevik or demented, and they fiercely opposed him.[210] Although Cipriani was white, he had vast support from the mobilized black population, who saw him as an interceding agent. Cipriani was, however, less successful with Indians, who were relatively isolated in plantations. Cipriani made no attempts to research the Indian masses on a person-to-person level; rather, he relied on radical Indian followers to mobilize them for the Trinidad Labour Party. Still, the vast majority of Indians did not identify with Captain Capriani's "national" movement.[211]

Next major populist leader was Urlah Butler, who was born in Granada around 1891. Butler was an expert agitator and was involved in left-wing politics. Butler was closer to the masses than was Capriani, and Butler was able to speak in the idiom of the masses. Butler was a good speaker, and the people of Trinidad were moved by his speeches. Ivar Oxaal describes the value of oratorical skills for Trinidadians: "West Indians place a high premium on linguistic skill; they are thoroughly versed in its ceremonial and oratorical variants and will listen with evident pleasure to any amount of long-winded speech-

---

[208] Oxaal, *Black Intellectuals Come to Power*, p. 50.
[209] Ryan, *Race and Nationalism in Trinidad and Tobago*, p. 35.
[210] Ryan, *Race and Nationalism in Trinidad and Tobago*, p. 36.
[211] Ryan, *Race and Nationalism in Trinidad and Tobago*, pp. 38-39.

making so long as it is apt and witty, and they will endure it in silence even when it is not."[212]

Butler's oratorical skills and Trinidadians' appreciation of that remind the readers of Chuck Ramkissoon in Joseph O'Neill's *Netherland*, who often make long-winded, albeit interesting, speeches. Joseph O'Neill captures a quintessential quality of Trinidad and its culture in the character of Chuck Ramkissoon.

And this quintessentially Trinidadian character of Butler drew Trinidadians to himself. Butler believed that God appointed him to lead the people of the West Indies away from colonialism. In a sense, Butler can be attributed with creating a Messianic element to black empowerment in Trinidad.[213] Butler founded his first political party, the British Empire Workers and Citizens Home Rule Party, in 1936. Butler accused Capriani of relying on his white friends and losing key battles for workers at important moments.[214]

The election of 1946 was the first election with universal suffrage and provided the new nationalism[215] forces to test their strength. A coalition was formed and called the United Front, and Jack Kelshall, a white creole veteran, was the driving force. Kelshall used the popular-strong strategy that was in vogue among left-wing groups in Europe. The United Front's manifesto declared itself as a "Socialist Front."[216]

The United Front's plan for nationalization received strong opposition from two places; namely, orthodox trade unionists and conservative businessmen. The Orthodox trade unionists did not like the strong socialist bent. The conservative

---

[212] Oxaal, *Black Intellectuals Come to Power*, p. 4.

[213] Oxaal, *Black Intellectuals Come to Power*, p. 100.

[214] Ryan, *Race and Nationalism in Trinidad and Tobago*, p. 46.

[215] Alvin Magid states: "Nationalism is a corollary of anticolonialism, that is, colonialism produces anticolonialism which, in turn, begets nationalism as a means of legitimizing opposition to a colonial situation marked by asymmetry in relations of power and authority" (Magid, *Urban Nationalism*, p. 12).

[216] Ryan, *Race and Nationalism in Trinidad and Tobago*, p. 74.

businessmen argued that since oil was a highly speculative industry, which required highly technical skills and marketing arrangements, a nationalized industry would not be efficient. These conservative businessmen argued that since Trinidad was small, it was vulnerable to international entities, which would force it to sell oil abroad at prices fixed by those international entities, if the oil industry were nationalized and less flexible for maneuvering.[217]

The election of 1946 witnessed mass mobilization like never before, and it was a heavily heated contest for nine available seats. Two primary factors were used to mobilize the inert masses: bribes and race.[218] Ryan states: "Every party and candidate accused the other of using them to gain electoral advantage."[219] Of the 259,512 eligible voters, only 137,281 (about 53%) voted. Some were turned off by overtly race-related political campaigning.

The election of 1950, in a sense, marked a break from the former colonialist system, since it was to produce a new constitution, which attempted to modify the colonialist system. The former constitution was still colonialist in that the Governor had predominant power. Furthermore, the power of the ministers was shared with Crown-appointed civil servants. And the ultimate power rested with the Crown.[220] The constitutional issues were reopened in 1955, and a few far-reaching suggestions were made, such as the creation of an Executive Council consisting of ten elected ministers. The Governor endorsed the suggestions of the Committee, although he recommended certain modifications relating to the size of the Executive Council; the Governor felt that there should be eight rather than ten elected ministers. The election of April, 1955, was postponed for the purposes of further debates on the new constitution. Furthermore, there was a widespread fear

---

[217] Ryan, *Race and Nationalism in Trinidad and Tobago*, p. 75.
[218] Ryan, *Race and Nationalism in Trinidad and Tobago*, p. 76.
[219] Ryan, *Race and Nationalism in Trinidad and Tobago*, p. 76.
[220] Ryan, *Race and Nationalism in Trinidad and Tobago*, p. 86.

among the majority of the population that the Hindu-based People's Democratic Party was likely to win the largest number of representatives if the elections were held in 1955, because the Hindus were the only well-organized group in the country. Ryan states: "Non-Indians considered the prospect of a Hindu-controlled government intolerable."[221]

During the election of 1950, Butler emerged as a clear winner in the sense that his political party, the Butler Party, won six seats on the new Council. Butler had formed the Butler Party after being released from detention in 1940, when Butler tried to regain his leadership of the working class movement and the Oilfield Workers Trade Union. Butler claimed that his own trade union was denying him power and glory due him, and Butler tried to engineer a strike which would destroy OWTU. Butler was detained again in 1941 for these activities. In 1946, Butler called a general strike and brought the economy to a standstill. His goal was similar to that of Cipriani and Rienzi before him, to form a "sugar and oil" coalition; that is, black oil workers with Indian sugar workers. In 1950, Butler forged a successful alliance of blacks and Indians. In fact, four of the six seats won by the Butler party were held by Indians.[222] In a sense, Chuck Ramkissoon and his marriage to a black Trinidadian typifies a type of Butler union on a social level. The alliance between Butler and Indian politicians quickly fell apart, however, in Trinidad because Indians saw Butler as an obstacle to Indian empowerment in Trinidad.[223]

In a sense, Chuck Ramkissoon having a lover on the side in his cricket games typifies the tenuous nature of the black-Indian alliance in Trinidad. In fact, Chuck Ramkissoon wants to be buried not in Trinidad, but rather in the USA. Chuck Ramkisson tells his black wife Anne in front of his friend Hans, "I want to rest here. In Brooklyn. Not Trinidad, not Long Island, not Queens" (p. 159). When his wife Anne does not react,

---

[221] Ryan, *Race and Nationalism in Trinidad and Tobago*, p. 101.
[222] Ryan, *Race and Nationalism in Trinidad and Tobago*, p. 89.
[223] Ryan, *Race and Nationalism in Trinidad and Tobago*, p. 91.

Chuck reiterates his wishes, "Did you hear me? In Brooklyn. A cremation, and then an interment of ashes" (p. 159). It is interesting to note that a typical burial ceremony in India involved cremation of the body. Thus, Chuck was harkening on his own Indian identity. Chuck did not feel belonging in Trinidad, and he felt that he had created his own homeland in Brooklyn. It was there he felt the most belonging.

In contrast, Chuck Ramkissoon's black wife wants to be buried in Trinidad. Blacks had a sense of belonging to Trinidad, whereas Indians felt foreign there. Anne Ramkissoon does not comprehend her husband's identity crisis. After his death, Anne decides to bury Chuck Ramkissoon in Trinidad, against her husband's own wishes. Anne Ramkissoon tells Hans, the narrator of *Netherland*, "My husband body going back to Trinidad. He is going to rest with his people" (p. 236). Anne Ramkissoon considered Chuck, her husband, to be a Trinidadian, but Chuck himself did not.

When Hans first meets Chuck and introduces himself as Hans van den Broek, Chuck asks if Hans is South African. Hans tells Chuck that he is from Holland and asks in turn where Chuck Ramkissoon is from. Chuck replies and says, "Here ... The United States" (p. 17). His girlfriend elbows him, and Chuck says to her, "What do you want me to say?" (p. 17). And the girlfriend replies, "Trinidad .... He's from Trinidad" (p. 17). This shows that Chuck Ramkissoon did not consider Trinidad as his home. For Chuck, Trinidad was foreign, and Chuck decided to make USA his home. The internal tension of Chuck Ramkissoon illustrates the internal tension of Indian politicians in Trinidad who did not feel totally home. They were trying to empower their minority people in the midst of the majority; they did not feel completely at home.

The friction between Indians and blacks of Trinidad was real. It was no accident that the election of 1955 was postponed to ensure that a Hindu-dominated government would not emerge in Trinidad. In fact, it was this fear of the minority ruling over the majority that captured the masses in a powerful nationalist movement that emerged in 1955-1956 in the form of People's National Movement (PNM).[224] Ryan describes:

> The dynamism and revolutionary idealism of the PNM was as challenging to those who were hungry for change and meaningful leadership as it was frightening to established elements in the society. Politically conservative Hindus, white settlers and businessmen, the Catholic Church, the old-line trade unions, and political leaders all feared its powerful hold over the Negro masses and did their utmost to undermine its influence. The election of 1956, seen by many as a conflict of two worlds – the old world of colonialism, racial snobbery, and corruption, and the new with its promise of integral decolonization – were the most critical that the country had yet witnessed. The victory of PNM brought to fruition the work of those who had struggled to create meaningful party politics in Trinidad and Tobago, and it appeared that the country had finally rid itself of its reputation in the Caribbean for political immaturity.[225]

In a sense, People's National Movement (PNM) was a black nationalism movement.

But PNM was not the only nationalist party in Trinidad. In fact, now a sizable Indian community formed their own nationalist party, the People's Democratic Party (PDP). Ryan states: "There is little doubt that soon after its foundation it became widely recognized as the political arm of the orthodox Hindu community, the vehicle of an Indian 'nationalist'

---

[224] The name was changed in 1956; the People's Education Movement became the People's National Movement (Oxaal, *Black Intellectuals Come to Power*, p. 137).

[225] Ryan, *Race and Nationalism in Trinidad and Tobago*, p. 103.

movement which paralleled the Negro-dominated People's National Movement."[226] In a sense, the black nationalist movement and Indian nationalist movement collided in Trinidad.

The leader of the Hindu nationalist party, the People's Democratic Party, was Bhadase Maraj, who was thought to be the wealthiest man in Trinidad. Bhadase Maraj quickly gained the reputation for being the greatest benefactor of the Hindu community. Bhadase Maraj was nicknamed, "Nehru of Trinidad."[227] Maraj told the Indians during the elections to vote as a block to vindicate their Indian forefathers who did not have the opportunity to vote.[228] Williams, the leader of PNM, developed a strategy to defeat the Hindu-centric People's Democratic Party. Williams was at an advantage because he had done much to raise attention to the Indian plight on social and economic levels in their plantation life in 19th and 20th centuries. In a speech on India's Republic Day in 1954, Williams endorsed the struggle of Indians to educate and improve itself. Ryan describes William's strategy: "The strategy, then, was to drive a wedge between orthodox Hindus on the one hand and the reformist Hindus, Moslems, and Christianized Indians on the other by portraying the PDP as an obscurantist communal organization."[229] Williams accomplished this in two ways. First, Williams linked Maha Sabha of Trinidad, which was a religious organization representing orthodox Hindus, to the fanatical Hindu Maha Sabha in India, which both Gandhi and Nehru denounced. Secondly, Williams represented People's Democratic Party as an economically conservative Brahmin party, which had nothing in common with the modern Indian secular nationalism of Tagore and Nehru, whom the Indian masses of Trinidad admired.[230]

---

[226] Ryan, *Race and Nationalism in Trinidad and Tobago*, p. 139.
[227] Ryan, *Race and Nationalism in Trinidad and Tobago*, p. 139.
[228] Ryan, *Race and Nationalism in Trinidad and Tobago*, p. 139.
[229] Ryan, *Race and Nationalism in Trinidad and Tobago*, p. 140.
[230] Ryan, *Race and Nationalism in Trinidad and Tobago*, p. 140.

It is interesting that Joseph O'Neill's Chuck Ramkissoon shares the last name with a historical figure of Trinidad, the Anglican Canon J. D. Ramkeesoon, whose letter was published in the *Guardian* in January, 1955. In this letter, the Anglican Canon J. D. Ramkeesoon praised Williams for an article he had written in commemoration of India's Republic Day, which stressed the common heritage of Indians and Negroes in the Caribbean.

The Anglican Canon J. D. Ramkeesoon was ethnically Indian.[231] There is high probability that Chuck Ramkissoon's name derived from this Indian clergy of the Anglican Church in Trinidad. In a sense, both Chuck Ramkissoon of Joseph O'Neill's novel and the Anglican Canon J. D. Ramkeesoon share another thing in common; both were betrayed. Chuck Ramkissoon was betrayed by his American Dream that he could make it in America; the dog-eat-dog world of American capitalism ended up killing Chuck Ramkissoon. And the Anglican Canon J. D. Ramkeesoon was betrayed by Williams, who in essence eventually became the chief architect of Indian disenfranchisement in Trinidad and Trinidadian politics; the Indian clergyman Ramkeesoon's ideal Dream also failed. Thus, Joseph O'Neill's use of the name of the historical figure in Trinidad must be seen as strategic and not accidental. Williams and the People's National Movement (PNM)'s rise to power was, in fact, a defeat for the Indians of Trinidad.

The People's National Movement (PNM) proved victorious in the election of September 24, where PNM captured thirteen of the twenty-four seats in the Legislative Council, which was the first time in history that a political party captured a majority of the elected offices. PNM had 39% of the total vote. The second most victorious political party was the Hindu-centerd People's Democratic Party with 20.3% of the votes and five seats in the Legislative Council. For many blacks in Trinidad, Williams was almost a Messianic figure. Oxaal states: "For many lower class Negroes, particularly Creole

---

[231] Oxaal, *Black Intellectuals Come to Power*, p. 107.

women, Dr. Williams was nothing less than a messiah come to lead the black children into the Promised Land."[232]

In the period from September 1956 to August 1962, there were a consolidation of power by the black-dominated People's National Movement and the rally of opponents, the Hindu and the European, in the Democratic Labour Party.[233] On April 1, 1958, Williams delivered a historic and far-reaching speech,[234] entitled, "The Dangers Facing Trinidad and Tobago and the West Indian Nation."

Williams accused Indians of playing race politics and pointed to the campaign letter addressed to "My dear Brother Indian" and signed "Yours truly Indian," which had been widely circulated in the countryside. The letter accused Williams of "favoring his own kind in the Cabinet" and of selecting "a few Indians to mislead other Indians into supporting his movement in order to have a majority." The letter concluded: "If, my dear brother, you have realized these occurrences, and the shaky position in which our Indian people are placed, woe unto our Indian nation in the next ten years."[235] Responding to this campaign letter, Williams retorted: "The Indian nation is in India."[236] Williams further accused the Indians of Trinidad of being "recalcitrant and hostile minority masquerading as the

---

[232] Oxaal, *Black Intellectuals Come to Power*, p. 100.

[233] Ryan, *Race and Nationalism in Trinidad and Tobago*, p. 171.

[234] Williams was a gifted speaker. Oxaal describes: "Dr. William's speeches in the University of Woodford Square sometimes have an *ex cathedra* quality. Thousands of lower-class auditors stand almost motionless for hours in the warm tropical night while the Doctor speaks in a carefully modulated, but still rather monotonous voice into the microphone on the square's Victorian bandstand" (Oxaal, *Black Intellectuals Come to Power*, p. 4). This explains the deep impact Williams had on the common masses of Trinidad, including his anti-Indian political programs.

[235] Ryan, *Race and Nationalism in Trinidad and Tobago*, p. 192.

[236] Ryan, *Race and Nationalism in Trinidad and Tobago*, p. 192.

Indian nation, and prostituting the name of India for its selfish, reactionary political ends."[237]

The government's systematic negative reaction against the Indian population became visible in the changing electoral rules leading to the 1961 elections. This may have been due to the realization that Indians were a larger population than had been previously thought. According to the 1960 Census of Trinidad and Tobago, there were 358,588 blacks in Trinidad and Tobago, or 43.3% of the population, and there were 301,946 Indians, which was 36.5% of the total population.[238] Indians were a sizable population that could potentially supplant the black population of Trinidad and Tobago.

In 1960, the Trinidad government introduced legislation for permanent voting registration. The Democratic Labour Party objected and stated that this may exploit certain segments of the population since the permanent voting registration would require carrying of a permanent identification card with a photograph and record of physical features and ethnic and religious background. Furthermore, the Democratic Labour Party stated that some 16% of the voting population, mostly poor, will stay away from the polls because the new permanent registration required literacy and many of the poor were illiterate. Since the illiteracy[239] rate was highest among the Indians in Trinidad, this new legislation would hurt the Indians the most.[240]

Furthermore, in the middle of 1961, another controversial legislation, called the Representation of the Peoples Ordinance, was published for public consumption. There were two particularly new measures; namely, the use of voting machines instead of the ballot box and the limitation on the size of campaign chests. Voting machines required

---

[237] Ryan, *Race and Nationalism in Trinidad and Tobago*, p. 192.
[238] Oxaal, *Black Intellectuals Come to Power*, p. 22.
[239] Compulsory primary school education was not fully implemented until the 1950s (Magid, *Urban Nationalism*, p. 216).
[240] Ryan, *Race and Nationalism in Trinidad and Tobago*, p. 239.

transportation vehicles for rural voters, and strict measures were taken to allow only one vehicle for two thousand voters. Due to the fear of multiple voting, the police were given wide latitude to impound cars suspected of violations. Since many Indians were in rural areas, the Democratic Labour Party objected to these measures; they argued that one car for two thousand voters was inadequate.[241]

In a sense, these measures targeting Indians, many of whom were in rural areas, were meant to maintain the dominance of the majority in Trinidad against the rising, powerful minority. The Democratic Labour Party also objected to the cap on $2,400 (TT) ceiling on campaign funds because it disadvantaged the minority, which depended on bigger campaign funds to win elections. Some have noted that one of the advantages of the Obama campaign against Hillary Clinton was that he had raised more campaign funds, and this played a role in his defeat of Hillary Clinton in the Democratic primaries. The Trinidad majority perceived the threat of election victory of the Indian minority due to greater campaign funds. Thus, the election of 1961 can be seen as representing the effort of the majority to impose a corrective on the political system, which had given unfair advantage to the minority. In a sense, the 1961 election represented an effort to subjugate the Indian minority under the majority of the population of Trinidad.[242]

Also, the black majority of Trinidad tried to use the permission by the Colonial Office to redraft electoral boundaries to its advantage. Although DLP wanted neutral persons from the West Indies or the United Kingdom to be in the commission to redraw electoral boundaries, the Colonial Office had authorized the Legislature to contribute dominantly to the new

---

[241] Ryan, *Race and Nationalism in Trinidad and Tobago*, p. 242.

[242] The Black Power movement of the 1960s can be seen as a descendant of the first Trinidad Workingmen's Association founded in 1897 by a small group of black artisans, who emphasized actions by the black laboring class, especially in Port-of-Spain and other mains towns. In a sense, the Black Power movement in Trinidad had always been an urban phenomena (Magid, *Urban Nationalism*, 243).

commission to redraw election lines. Thus, the black majority and its political party PNM guided the direction on the redrawing of the electoral boundaries, since the new commission created for that purpose had three PNM party members and a judge who was also thought to be a PNM party member. Only one member of the commission belonged to the Opposition.

The commission gave one electoral seat for as few as 11,492 voters in urban areas, where the black majority dominated, but gave one electoral seat for as many as 12,735 voters in the rural areas, dominated by Indian voters.[243] This would obviously decrease the power of Indians in Trinidad, who tended to blockvote along racial lines. Ryan states: "The debate on the report of the commission provides extremely rich evidence in support of our fundamental thesis, *that ethnicity is the dominant variable in the political life of Trinidad and Tobago.*"[244]

It is not surprising that in light of such maneuver by the black majority against the Indian minority that Chuck Ramkissoon, who is Indian, did not want to be buried in Trinidad and did not consider himself really as a Trinidadian, but as an American. Chuck Ramkissoon did not consider Trinidad as his real homeland. There were many Indians who reacted strongly to PNM's efforts to disenfranchise Indian votes, and some were quite militant. Oxaal's first-person observation of Indian militancy in 1961 elections provides a picture into the sentiments of Indians in Trinidad:

> On a lovely Sunday afternoon in October, 1961, I sat among a group of D.L.P. dignitaries while, on the platform a few feet away, Dr. Rudranath Capildeo cried out to a gathering of 30,000 East Indians standing on the Savannah to "arm yourselves with weapons and get ready to take

---

[243] Ryan, *Race and Nationalism in Trinidad and Tobago*, p. 244.
[244] Ryan, *Race and Nationalism in Trinidad and Tobago*, p. 244.

over the government of this country." A few weeks before, he had exhorted his followers to smash the voting machines which the P.N.M. government was installing for the December elections. The dominant tone of the D.L.P. campaign was one of fear and hysteria; it was impossible for an outsider – as I was then – to comprehend the self-defeating tactics which Dr. Capildeo employed. It was evident, however, that there was a deep, non-rational bond between this troubled genius and his followers; but, like most non-Indians in Trinidad the nature of that communion was obscure to me.[245]

It is clear that the election of 1961 was racially charged election, and some perceived it as a battle between the black majority and the Indian minority.

The race element was so strong leading into the 1961 elections that Williams had to warn PNM party members to "stop once and for all this infuriating nonsense that every Indian is anti-PNM. …. Some of the worst enemies of the PNM are as black as the ace of spades. …. A PNM Indian, trustworthy, loyal, devoted to the PNM, is a thousand times a better citizen than an anti-PNM African."[246] Obviously, this was a political statement made in order to keep Indian members of PNM loyal and to shame blacks who did not support PNM. The actions of PNM, especially related to electoral reforms, show that Williams was interested in disenfranchising the Indian population of Trinidad. Even if such actions were motivated by party politics, it does not change the fact that it, in fact, disenfranchised Indians, most of whom belonged to the opposition party.

Ironically, the opposition made some fatal flaws in the election of 1961 that might have done more damage to its own

---

[245] Oxaal, *Black Intellectuals Come to Power*, p. 159.
[246] Ryan, *Race and Nationalism in Trinidad and Tobago*, p. 249.

victory. In the 1961 elections, the Democratic Labour Party did all it could to portray itself as a non-Hindu party and a party of all peoples.

> While it is true that all the Hindu candidates were given safe rural constituencies, two such constituencies were given to Negroes and another to a Moslem. The DLP thus felt quite justified in its boast that it was 'a miniature United Nations, a rally of all creeds, races, and walks of life.' It had leaned over backwards to prove to all that it was not a mere Hindu faction.[247]

In a sense, DLP had succumbed to the polemic of PNM against it and diluted Indian power within DLP. And as a result the Democratic Labour Party suffered a disastrous defeat in the elections. DLP only won 10 seats out of 30 possible seats. Election results showed that PNM made headway into presumably Indian strongholds. The political leader of DLP declared: "We did not fight an election. We simply went through the motions of a monstrous farce. …. PNM has found a way to win elections without popular support."[248] The method that PNM used to win was racial politics against Indians. And the political leader of DLP was wrong; PNM had popular support. In fact, PNM won 58% of the popular vote, so no one could accuse PNM any longer of being a minority government.[249]

PNM won 20 seats out of 30 possible seats. When PNM formed the government, their anti-Hindu bias was clear; PNM allowed no Hindu to sit in the Cabinet. Of the twelve Cabinet spots, eight went to blacks, two to those of European descent,

---

[247] Ryan, *Race and Nationalism in Trinidad and Tobago*, p. 255.
[248] Ryan, *Race and Nationalism in Trinidad and Tobago*, p. 282.
[249] Ryan, *Race and Nationalism in Trinidad and Tobago*, pp. 282-283.

and two to Muslims.[250] Obviously, by appointing two Muslim Indians to the Cabinet, PNM was hoping to dilute the Hindu influence and Hindu power even among the Indians. Blacks in Trinidad effectively disenfranchised the Hindu minority which was rising to power in Trinidad through aggressive racial politics coupled with a dissembling façade of multiculturalism. The fact that Hindus tried to embrace multiculturalism in response to the politically motivated attacks of PNM, in essence, contributed to their crippling defeat in the elections, even in areas where Hindus were dominant. PNM effectively wrested many Hindu votes away from the Democratic Labour Party, which was no longer Hindu-centric. Politically, the Hindu-party had cut its own throat by excising aggressive pro-Hindu element away from the party, thereby losing its own electoral base to the enemy party.

Once in power, PNM systematically cut down Hindu power. Ryan describes: "Despite his genuine intellectual commitment to multiracialism, he refused to concede minority communities the right to elect their own kind, or to articulate their own version of the national community. The majoritarian thesis implicitly promised a homogeneous society, a non-racial rather than multiracial society."[251] Thus, the perceived minority threat propelled the leaders of the majority to an aggressive program of disenfranchisement of the Hindu minority, which had amassed much power and influence. In fact, Williams believed in an inverse relationship between black empowerment and the power of the minorities. Ryan describes: "William believed that he had a responsibility to emancipate the Negro, to stimulate in him pride, dignity, and a feeling of independence, and that his goal necessitated an attack, however subtly concealed, on the European and Indian communities."[252] In other words, black power could not co-

---

[250] Ryan, *Race and Nationalism in Trinidad and Tobago*, p. 290.
[251] Ryan, *Race and Nationalism in Trinidad and Tobago*, p. 375.
[252] Ryan, *Race and Nationalism in Trinidad and Tobago*, p. 376.

exist; there had to be an attack on the groups who posed threat to its dominance.

With the historic and revolutionary election victory of 1961, PNM decided to take Trinidad to independence alone and published on May 9, 1962, a "draft independence constitution."[253] This was obviously the natural corollary to black victory of the government; all other powers that posed a threat to the black nationalism of Trinidad had to be diminished, including that of the colonialist power.

In a sense, Chuck Ramkissoon of Joseph O'Neill was shaped by the historical force of Trinidad's history. Chuck Ramkissoon was a Tridadian of Indian descent whose Indian parents had experienced the disenfranchisement of the Indian community in Trinidad through shrewd political maneuverings of the black-centered political party. Chuck Ramkissoon had experienced what many Indians in Trinidad saw as injustices for Indians of Trinidad. Thus, it is not surprising why Chuck Ramkissoon is so patriotic to America; he sees himself as American and believes that all is possible in America, in contrast to Trinidad. Chuck Ramkissoon's entrepreneurial ambitions were, in a sense, a type of faith in the American system, in American capitalism. Chuck Ramkissoon, in essence, was a true believer of American capitalism.

That is why Chuck Ramkisoon's death opening the novel, *Netherland*, is so significant. Here is this ideal immigrant who is a patriot and believes in the system, and it is this very immigrant who ends tragically dead. The primary thesis, insofar as Chuck Ramkissoon is involved, is that American capitalism betrays even its most loyal adherents, or that American capitalism is fundamentally evil.

The novel starts with the news of Chuck Ramkissoon's brutal murder and it ends on the same note. The use of a Trinidadian as the victim of American capitalism is historically and strategically significant in light of the history of Trinidad and the nature of Trinidad's politics. In a sense, the injustice in

---

[253] Ryan, *Race and Nationalism in Trinidad and Tobago*, p. 314.

Netherland by Joseph O'Neill & President Barak Obama's AMERICA

America is no different from the third world country from which Chuck Ramkissoon had escaped. The novel ends in the suspicion that Trinidad might have treated Chuck Ramkissoon better than American capitalism. This suspicion is confirmed in the fact that the "happy end" is the return of Hans the narrator, back home in London, England, away from America and New York City.

Netherland by Joseph O'Neill & President Barak Obama's AMERICA

"Abelsky and Shylock the Jew"

The novel, *Netherland*, by Joseph O'Neill provides a Shylock figure in the person of Mikhail Abelsky, or more commonly known as Mike Abelsky. In *The Merchant of Venice* by William Shakespeare, Shylock is a banker who could have taken the life of a Christian, named Antonio. In *Netherland*, Abelsky is a Shylock figure who is portrayed as likely having taken the life of a Christian, named Chuck Ramkissoon. In *The Merchant of Venice*, Shylock the banker represents the evils of capitalism. Debt can be a killer, and bankers have power over the lives of those who borrow from the bank. However, because the society was a Christian society, Shylock the banker could not succeed in his evil scheme. On the other hand, American capitalism is seen as wholly unruly and uncontrollable, under the manipulative power of Shylocks. The American financial crisis of 2008-2010 is a form of American banking crisis that is an evidence for the chaos of American capitalism, subjected to the manipulations of the banking industry.

Just as in *The Merchant of Venice*, *Netherland* presents a key economic element to the story that is shady and represents what is wrong with the society's economic system. In both systems, Jews are seen as having too much influence on the economic direction of entrepreneurs. Furthermore, both literary works share the idea that a Jew can pose a threat not only to business but to one's life. In *Netherland*, Abelsky, who is supposed to be Chuck Ramkissoon's partner and friend, is suspected of killing Chuck Ramkissoon for money. This is clear to the readers when Abelsky and Hans have a conversation about Chuck's death. Hans telephones Abelsky from England. The very first thing that Abelsky tells Hans seems like a type of confession. Abelsky says, "When he disappears, … a guy says to me, Maybe he killed himself. I said, You idiot! Chuck isn't a suicide guy! This guy has more life inside him than ten people! Then they find him in the river with his hands tied up. I tell this schmuck, I tell him, You see? I was right" (pages 230-231). Abelsky takes greater pride in being right than about Abelsky's death. The fact that Abelsky portrays himself as someone who does not know what had happened to Chuck during the period of Chuck's disappearance indicates that he wants to exonerate himself of the guilt of murder. But in a sense, it is a proud confession of someone who had committed the murderous act. When Abelsky states that Chuck had more life inside him than ten people, Abelsky is giving himself the credit for having killed Chuck. It is like someone describing his opponent as a Goliath, because that adds to the magnitude of the accomplishment.

What further implicates Abelsky is the comment that he makes soon after, "They never said what he died for." It is a comment that someone in the know makes about others who don't know; it is a way to make himself seem superior to the others. In effect, it is like stating, "They are too stupid to know what I had done to Chuck and why." But the motive for Abelsky's murder of Chuck seems to be money. When Hans asks, "What is happening to her share of the business?" (page 231), Abelsky pauses and says, "The lawyers are investigating all of this. She will get what she is entitled, of course" (page 231). This shows that Abelsky was not planning to give any money to Anne Ramkissoon, Chuck's wife. Abelsky was making excuses, in oder to get rid of Hans' suspicions. Hans understands the tactic and says, "Yes, she will" (page 231). This was meant as a form of a threat, and Abelsky understands it as such. Abelsky replies in Anger, "Otherwise what? .... Otherwise what? What gave you the right to talk?" (page 231). Abelsky threatens Hans because he has acquired bravado after having Chuck killed; he felt like he was invincible.

Abelsky further implicates himself in the murder of Chuck when he says flat out, "You think I killed him? You think I killed Chuck? What the hell! .... Because I'm a Russian, I kill him? Because I yell at the guy? Always we are fighting! From the beginning, when he told me how to sell kosher fish to the Jews. What a guy!" (page 231). In a sense, Abelsky "protests too much." Abelsky is trying to make himself look innocent of Chuck's death by feigning hurt and anger at the possible suggestion. Of course, the important fact is that Hans did not make any such accusation. In a MacBethian fashion, Abelsky was talking to an imaginary accuser, as his guilt weighed heavily on him. Here, one sees another possible motive, besides money, for which Abelsky had Chuck killed. Abelsky seems grossly offended that Chuck, a non-Jew, had told him, a religious Jew, how to sell kosher fish to the Jews. It was a hurt that was deeply personal, and the hurt was against Abelsky's sense of group identity. It was a way of Abelsky saying, "How dare a Gentile tell Jews how to sell Jewish stuff to Jews?" It was an ethnic-religious insult that could have been a justification in Abselsky's mind for having Chuck killed. In this sense, Abelsky is very similar to Shylock the Jew in Shakespeare's *The Merchant of Venice*, who took serious offense at the way Christians treated him.

Like Chuck of *Netherland*, Shylock of *The Merchant of Venice* seems fixated on how badly Christians treat him, a Jew, and his people, the Jews. Shylock sensitively tells Antonio, "You call me misbeliever, cut-throat dog. And spit upon my Jewish garberdine, And all for use of that which is mine one" (Act 1, Scene 3). Shylock the Jew has an axe to grind against Christians. This is nowhere more evident than in Shylock's famous soliloquy:

> To bait fish withal: if it will feed nothing else, it will feed my revenge. He hath disgraced me, and hindered me half a million; laughed at my losses, mocked at my gains, scorned my nation, thwarted my bargains, cooled my friends, heated mine enemies; and what's his reason? I am a Jew. Hath not a Jew eyes? Hath not a Jew hands, organs, dimensions, senses, affections, passions? Fed with the same food, hurt with

> the same weapons, subject to the same diseases, healed by the same means, warmed and cooled by the same winter and summer, as a Christian is? If you prick us, do we not bleed? If you tickle us, do we not laugh? If you poison us, do we not die? And if you wrong us, shall we not revenge? If we are like you in the rest, we will resemble you in that. If a Jew wrong a Christian, what is his humility? Revenge. If a Christian wrong a Jew, what should his sufferance be by Christian example? Why, revenge. The villainy you teach me, I will execute; and it shall go hard but I will better the instruction (Act 3, Scene 1).

It is clear that Shylock is filled with hatred for Christians and a desire to take revenge for what he perceives as a wrong committed against him as a Jew. This is the same kind of murderous hatred that Abelsky, in essence, confesses at a perceived wrong against him and his fellow Jews.

It is this sectarian hatred that propels Shylock to desire the death of Antonio and to create a requirement of a pound of flesh as the bond for the loan. Shylock the Jew says, "This kindness will I show. Go with me to a notary, seal me there Your single bond; and, in a merry sport, If you repay me not on such a day, In such a place, such sum or sums as are Express'd in the condition, let the forfeit Be nominated for an equal pound Of your fair flesh, to be cut off and taken In whatever part of your body pleaseth me" (Act 1, Scene 3). In a sense, Shylock the Jew was slyly setting up Antonio the Christian to be killed by the instrument of the court of law. This is nowhere clearer than in Shylock the Jew's first statement in the court demanding the death of Antonio:

> I have possess'd your Grace of what I purpose
> And by our holy Sabbath have I sworn
> To have the due and forfeit of my bond:

> If you deny it, let the danger light
> Upon your charter and your city's freedom.
> You'll ask me, why I rather choose to have
> A weight of carrion-flesh than to receive
> Three thousand ducats: I'll not answer that:
> But say, it is my humour: is it answer'd?
> What if my house be troubled with a rat,
> And I be pleased to give ten thousand ducats
> To have it baned? What, are you answer'd yet?
> (Act 4, Scene 1).

Shylock the Jew is willing to curse the city and the city's liberty in order to ensure the death of a Christian.

This is reminiscent of the death that the Jews during the time of Jesus of Nazareth sought. Jews wanted Jesus of Nazareth dead, because of the slight they felt he aimed at them. Thus, Shylock the Jew takes on the type of Jews of the Gospels, and Antonio takes the type of Jesus of Nazareth, who selflessly gave himself up for the salvation of others, which in the case of *The Merchant of Venice* is Bassanio, who received salvation in marriage to Portia as the result of Antonio's self-sacrifice. Shylock the Jew repeats again to the court his desire to have Antonio killed: "Till thou canst rail the seal from off my bond, Thou but offend'st thy lungs to speak so loud: Repair thy wit, good youth, or it will fall To cureless ruin. I stand here for law" (Act 4, Scene 1). Shylock the Jew was seeking the force of the law for the death of Antonio, and in this, Shylock the Jew fits the stereotype of Jews in the Bible as legalistic and Pharisaic. Thus, Shylock the Jew typifies the Law as Jews of the Gospels do, and opposed to Grace, which Jesus Christ typifies.

Antonio was saved from legalistic Shylock the Jew, because the society was fundamentally Christian, and there were Christians willing to save Antonio. If Jews had been dominant and had there been Jewish justices and judges, Antonio would most likely have ended up in prison in the least, or in death as Shylock the Jew preferred. Shakespeare's *The Merchant of Venice*, in a way, is therefore a warning to

Christians in his society that it would be dangerous to allow Jews to hold positions of authority in the government or in the court system. The social impact of the message of *The Merchant of Venice* by Shakespeare must have been immense on the English psyche, for even now, no one who is not a Christian can become the Prime Minister of the United Kingdom. The political and legal power in the UK is firmly in the hands of those who consider themselves as Christians. In contrast to a proactively Christian society which protects Antonio in *The Merchant of Venice*, Chuck Ramkissoon of *Netherland* suffers death at the hands of Abelsky the Jew because New York City is fundamentally non-Christian, as the city with the greatest inhabitants of Jews in the world, and the Christian Chuck dies a horrific death, bound, as Jesus of Nazareth was on the cross in another time in a city with Jewish dominance. Thus, Chuck Ramkissoon is a type of Jesus Christ. Abelsky's mention of lawyers highlights the legalistic stereotype of Jews throughout history, since the Gospel accounts.

In *Netherland*, New York City is portrayed as dominated by Jews. Thus, Chuck Ramkissoon describes the impossibility of doing business without some Jewish connection. Chuck Ramkissoon tells Hans, "I knew there was money to be made. I foresaw the Brooklyn boom, Hans. I saw it as clearly as you see me now. I focused on Williamsburg, which was full of the kind of run-down commercial buildings I wanted, buildings with high profit potential. But they were owned by Jews. I had no access" (pages 134). Chuck Ramkissoon found the way to overcome the obstacle by getting a Jewish frontman to be the face of his companies. Chuck Ramkissoon tells Hans, "So I hooked up with Abelsky. I met him at the Russian baths, this big fat guy who never stopped moaning. ..... That's why I went to the baths in the first place, to meet Jews. Where else was I going to meet them?" (page 134). After meeting Abelsky the Jew, Chuck Ramkissoon started running his business as if Abelsky were in charge, but Abelsky was only the frontman. Chuck Ramkissoon describes:

> So I set up a real estate company with Abelsky and I cut him in for twenty-five points to be my frontman. Of course, I took care of everything. Abelsky's job was to stay in the background and act like a big shot too busy to handle the details. And listen to him today: he actually thinks he is a big shot! When all he's ever done is lend me his Jewish name! .... Our sushi business? Abelsky & Co. The real estate company? Abelsky Real Estate Corporation (page 134).

Obviously, the readers are feeling frustration at this decision by Chuck Ramkissoon, since that was more than motive enough for Abelsky to have Chuck killed. When Hans and Abelsky talks after Chuck's body is discovered, Abelsky tells Hans, "He was a great employee. Full of ideas. Although I should have fired his ass a hundred times. I'm paying his salary and he sets up an office in the city? With no one else I would have allowed this! Nobody! Only Chuck!" (page 231). Obviously this is a lie, as the description of Chuck as a mere employee does not fit the character of Chuck as an active leader in every setting.

Furthermore, Abelsky's identity as the frontman fits the description of Abelsky throughout the story. Chuck Ramkissoon describes the reason why he picked Abelsky as his frontman. Abelsky was not liked by anyone, so Chuck thought he would be willing to work with a colored man. Chuck says,

> A disaster area. Nobody at the baths wanted to talk to him. Nobody wanted to whack him with the twigs. 'Come on, guys, give me a break. Dimitri, I'm begging you. Boris – come on, Boris. Please. Just a few whacks.' No. They wouldn't go near him. .... I'm telling you, those Russian guys preferred my company. And believe me, they weren't happy having me around. Anyhow, I look at this guy, this pariah,

Netherland by Joseph O'Neill & President Barak Obama's AMERICA

and I say to myself, here's a guy who's so desperate he'd work with a coolie" (page 134).

There are too many details in Chuck Ramkissoon's story to make the recounting spurious, at least to the readers' minds. The consistency of Chuck Ramkissoon's description vis-à-vis Abelsky is maintained throughout *Netherland*. Hans as the narrator describes that Chuck Ramkissoon ignored the frequent calls by Abelsky. In the narrative, Chuck Ramkissoon is remembered as saying, "I've made this man this rich ... and this is what I have to put up with. You know when I met him he was driving a limousine? A bum from Moldova who couldn't wipe his own caca-hole" (page 162). The description of Abelsky as a dolt who would do anything for money fits Abelsky's character in other parts of the novel. Abelsky tells Hans and Chuck at the American steam room:

> I used to take beatings for my brothers. .... If my big brother scratched the car, he paid me to take the beating. My father was aware about what was going on, but still he would beat me. He used to beat the shit out of me. I laughed in his face. He couldn't get to me. He could beat me and beat me, but still I would laugh. What did I care? I was rich (page 143).

Clearly, Abelsky is the kind of character who would do anything for money. Furthermore, unlike Chuck Ramkissoon, Abelsky did not have the conception that he should work hard for money. Abelsky continues and expounds his philosophy for getting rich: "You wanna be rich in this country, you gotta win the Mega" (page 143). Winning the lottery was Abelsky's plan for getting rich. Certainly, Abelsky does not talk like an entrepreneur, whereas Chuck Ramkissoon does. Abelsky fits the image of a violent guy who is capable of murder. Abelsky also tells Hans and Chuck at the American steam room, "Once I was a wrestler. ..... Yeah, in the Russian army. Also at home, with my brothers.

I beat the shit out of them" (page 143). Mikhail Abelsky seems to be proud about his violent nature. Thus, the readers can understand that it was Abelsky who had Chuck killed.

Abelsky is a religious Jew, but his character is certainly capable of killing Chuck Ramkissoon. In one part of the novel, Mike Abelsky, who is a religious Jew, wearing the typical orthodox Jewish garb that religious Jews wear, carries a baseball bat with intent to hurt or threaten. Hans the narrator describes, "I was coming out of the deli when Abelsky, in Judaic[254] white shirt and black trousers, waddled by. To be accurate: I saw a baseball bat first, carried in a man's hand. Only then was I moved to recognize Abelsky" (page 213).

Those who have been to New York City, especially to Brooklyn, know what the "Judaic white shirt and black trousers" are; they are typical of the daily clothing worn by orthodox Jews not only in New York, but in Israel, France, England, Australia, all over the world. Thus, there is no equivocation about the orthodox Jewish identity of Abelsky; Abelsky wore the clothes of an orthodox Jew and thus is identified as an orthodox Jew. The identification is intentional. The contrast between his orthodox Jewish garb and the baseball bat[255] that he is carrying is

---

[254] The choice of the word "Judaic" is significant. Joseph O'Neill, the author of *Netherland*, could have used the word "Jewish," which is more common, but does not. Technically, "Judaic" is seen to relate to the religious nature of Judaism (and can be seen as the adjective form of "Judaism") more than "Jewish," although in the popular discourse in the United States, "Jewish" can have the same force of the meaning, "belonging to the Jewish religion, or Judaism."

[255] The fact that the instrument of violence is a baseball bat is significant. Since the novel criticizes American capitalism as chaotic and violent, it fits the theme of the novel to have the symbol that is quintessentially American (baseball or baseball bat) used as an instrument of violence. It points to the corruption and the corruptibility of the American capitalist system. The fact that the instrument of quintessentially American pastime is used as an instrument of violence in the hands of a religious Jew may be seen as strategic, given the similarities between Shylock the Jew from *The Merchant of Venice* and Mikhail Abelsky in *Netherland*.

obvious. Here was an orthodox religious Jew, who was carrying an instrument of torture and death (in the context of the story). Since Mike Abelsky is a Shylock figure in *Netherland*, the contrast is not so surprising.

In *The Merchant of Venice*, Shylock is an orthodox religious Jew, who is also prone to violence, torture, and murder. Shylock the Jew attends a synagogue and makes that place of Jewish religious gathering his regular meeting place. Shylock the Jew tells his Jewish friend Tubal, "Go, go Tubal, and meet me at our synagogue; go, good Tubal; at our synagogue, Tubal" (Act 3, Scene 1). Obviously, regular attendance at a synagogue is evidence of a person's Jewish religiosity. And Shylock the Jew observes kosher laws and thus refuses to eat with Bassanio. Shylock the Jew tells Bassanio, "Yes, to smell pork ... but I will not eat with you..." (Act 1, Scene 3). Like Mike Abelsky, who wore the Judaic clothing, Shylock the Jew wore a Judaic clothing, the gaberdine. Gaberdine was a long frock worn by Jews in the Middle Ages. It is clear that Shylock wears the Judaic attire in his accusation that Antonio spat at it. Shylock the Jew attacks Antonio, "You call me misbeliever, cut-throat dog, And spit upon my Jewish gabardine..." (Act 1, Scene 3).

Obviously, Mike Abelsky is described as wearing the Jewish outfit because he is a type of Shylock in modern-day America. Thus, Shylock the Jew, like Mike Abelsky, wore the Judaic religious garb. And like Mike Abelsky, Shylock the Jew was prone to violence. First of all, Shylock the Jew wanted to have Antonio killed, so he made the security of the loan a pound of Antonio's flesh. Shylock the Jew tells Antonio:

> This kindness will I show.
> Go with me to a notary, seal me there
> Your single bond; and, in a merry sport,[256]

---

[256] Shylock the Jew calling the bond arrangement meant to kill Antonio, "a merry sport," corresponds to Mike Abelsky's use of the

> If you repay me not on such a day,
> In such a place, such sum or sums as are
> Express'd in the condition, let the forfeit
> Be nominated for an equal pound
> Of your fair flesh, to be cut off and taken
> In what part of your body pleaseth me (Act 1, Scene 3).

This suggestion itself is violent and murderous. The bond's primary intent is to take advantage of Antonio's misfortune to have him killed. It is clear that Shylock the Jew was hoping for Antonio's death, when he exults at Antonio's business failings; Shylock the Jew looks forward to having Antonio tortured and killed. When Tubal, Shylock's Jewish friend, informs Shylock the Jew that Antonio's trade ship coming from Tripolis was wrecked and Antonio's fortune lost, Shylock the Jew celebrates and says, "I thank God, I thank God! Is 't true, is 't true?" (Act 3, Scene 1). Shylock could not contain his joy at the loss of Antonio, and continues, "I thank thee, good Tubal: good news, good news! Ha, ha!" (Act 3, Scene 1). And Shylock the Jew resolves to torture Antonio, "I am very glad of it: I'll plague him; I'll torture him: I am glad of it" (Act 3, Scene 1). Shylock the Jew enjoyed seeing the misfortune of Antonio, because it gave him the opportunity to torture him. Mike Abelsky is similar.

In *Netherland*, Mike Abelsky seizes the opportunity of someone's misfortune to torture him. Carrying a baseball bat and wearing his Judaic clothing, Mike Abelsky went into Focus Language School building somewhere in Williamsburg. Apparently, Abelsky went in to rough up someone, because when Hans entered the building, he found the room disheveled. A flower pot was broken, and a man had apparently been roughed up. Hans the narrator describes the room, "The office, a windowless box, was more or less destroyed. A filing cabinet had been upended and its contents were strewn everywhere. A

---

instrument of "a merry sport" for violence and torture. The correlation must be seen as significant.

framed map of the United States lay on the floor, its glass in pieces. Somebody had smashed a potted plant against the photocopying machine" (page 214). Apparently, Mike Abelsky with his bat had done this. Hans describes the smoking gun, "The baseball bat was resting against a wall. It was stained with dirt" (page 214). The victim was a man in his thirties. Hans describes, "A toilet flushed, and moments later the flusher, a man in his thirties, came in. He had splashed water on his face, but there were traces of soil around his ears and in his hair, which was of the pale, almost colorless, Russian variety. His blue shirt was filthy" (page 214). The description by Hans the narrator is similar to a description of the crime scene. In fact, Hans was traumatized by what he saw as perpetration of violence. Hans describes the feeling that went through when he experienced the trauma:

> Now the meaning of what I'd seen – Chuck and Abelsky had terrorized some unfortunate, smashed up his office, shoved his face in the dirt of a flowerpot, threatened him with worse for all I knew – arrived as a pure nauseant. I almost threw up then and there, at the feet of the gnome. I dropped my head between my knees, sucking in air. It took an effort of will to get up and go onward to a subway stop. Violence produces reactions of this kind, apparently (page 215).

But it was not really Chuck and Abelsky; it was just Abelsky with his bat who had terrorized the "unfortunate." Chuck was most likely just a bystander; violence did not fit Chuck's character.

In fact, Chuck is often described as a peace-maker. During one cricket game, a guy went to his car and got a gun. He brought disturbance to the whole field, and many people were afraid. Hans describes,

Netherland by Joseph O'Neill & President Barak Obama's AMERICA

> My eye was drawn to a figure walking slowly in the direction of the parked cars. I kept watching him because there was something mysterious about this person choosing to leave at such a moment of drama. He was in no hurry, it seemed. He slowly opened the door of a car, leaned in, reached around for a few moments, then stood up straight and shut the door. He appeared to be holding something in his hand as he strolled back into the grounds. People started shouting and running. A woman screamed. My teammates, grouped on the boundary, set off in every direction, some into the tennis courts, others to hide behind trees. Now the man was ambling over somewhat uncertainly. It occurred to me he was very drunk (page 13).

What the drunk man was holding was a gun, and he was pointing it at Chuck Ramkissoon. Hans describes, "The man stopped ten feet from Chuck. He held the gun limply. He looked at me, then back at Chuck. He was speechless and sweating. He was trying, as Chuck would afterward relate, to understand the logic of his situation" (page 14). Obviously, such a situation would unnerve most people, as was seen by the panic of the crowd. Even the narrator was seized with fear. Hans the narrator describes, "I felt nothing. I experienced the occasion as a kind of emptiness" (page 13). In other words, Hans' mind went numb, and he was immobilized. The situation was chaotic and filled with danger. And it was Chuck who was the peacemaker, who brought safety back to the cricket field. Hans describes Chuck's bravery: "Chuck took a step forward. 'Leave the field of play, sir,' he said firmly. He extended his palm towards the clubhouse, an usher's gesture. 'Leave immediately please. You are interfering with play'" (page 14). Chuck successfully calmed the gunman, and all went back to normal. In a sense, therefore, Chuck Ramkissoon was everyone's savior; he prevented any life from being lost. Chuck was not violent and is not described as violent in anything that Hans experienced with him or observed. Chuck was a peacemaker who made others' lives better, and thus Chuck is the direct foil of Mike Abelsky, who made others' lives worse and was prone to violence. Thus, it is not surprising that Hans van den Broek was drawn to Chuck Ramkissoon.

In fact, Hans van den Broek regards Chuck Ramkissoon as his friend. Hans admits, "It's true that I did not make inquiries into the deeper goings-on of Chuck Ramkissoon. It's also true that Chuck was a friend, not an anthropological curiosity" (page 167). Rachel, Hans' wife, does not believe that Hans was really Chuck's friend. Rachel accuses her husband: "You never really wanted to know him. .... You were just happy to play with him. Same thing with America. You're like a child. You don't look beneath the surface" (page 166). But more often than not, males tend to socialize on superficial levels. Males watch football together over pizza; they don't sit around trying to talk to each other to understand each other's feelings. Historically, that's not how men have socialized. And, in fact, Rachel is wrong. Hans knew a lot about Chuck, because Chuck made himself known. Chuck shared with Hans his life's dream, to build a cricket field. Chuck shared with him his difficulties as an immigrant. Chuck introduced Hans to his wife and invited him into his home. Chuck helped Hans with his driving test. Hans knew Chuck more than a typical male knows his male friends over many, many years. So, Rachel is mistaken to think that Hans did not know Chuck.

Interestingly enough, Hans does not seem to realize how much he knows Chuck, even after all they have been through and all that Chuck has shared with him. Although Hans did not "make inquiries into the deeper goings-on" of his friend, Hans knew Chuck as well as any male individual knows his best friend. There was really no aspect of Chuck Ramkissoon that Hans did not know at least in some way. Perhaps, Hans fell into the mistake that his wife Rachel fell into of assuming that people of different backgrounds could not be friends. Rachel proclaims to Hans, "You were two completely different people from different backgrounds. You had nothing important in common" (page 166). The assumption that people of different backgrounds could not be friends is faulty. The fact is that Hans and Chuck spent a lot of their social time together as friends. And Hans and Chuck have something very important in common; that is, cricket.

In fact, it was Rachel and Hans, who did not really know each other, even though they were a married couple. Hans did not even know when Rachel had fallen in love with him. This is the kind of a thing that married couples know before being married. But it is only after a week after the birth of their child, Jake, that Hans finds out. Rachel asks Hans, "Do you want to know exactly when I fell in love with you?" (page 199). Hans the narrator reflects, "I wanted to know about the moment my wife fell in love with me" (page 199). And Hans' wife Rachel tells him, "Remember when you told me about being in that boat at night, when you were little? That's when I fell in love with you. When you told me that story. At that exact moment" (page 199). This is not the only time that Hans seems to be ignorant of something about his wife that husbands are expected to know.

Even after Jake is grown up, Hans discovers things about his wife that a husband should know before marriage, such as Rachel being lactose intolerant. Hans describes, "It's possible that this fantasy originated in a revelation Rachel made one Saturday when she and Jake and I were shopping in Sainsbury's. She'd piled multiple cartons of soymilk into the cart, and this puzzled me. 'I am lactose intolerant,' Rachel explained. 'Since when?' I said. 'Since forever,' she said, 'You remember how I always had stomach cramps? That was the lactose" (page 125). This ignorance about his wife in something he should have known causes Hans to fantasize about intimacy with his wife, in which he and she would "have hours-long, disinterested, beans-spilling, let-the-chips-fall-where-they-may conversations in which we'd examine each other's unknown nooks and crannies in the best of humor and faith" (page 125). This is a fantasy for

Netherland by Joseph O'Neill & President Barak Obama's AMERICA

intimacy and love. Apparently, Hans and Rachel lack intimacy and love that should exist between a husband and a wife.

Hans describes the lack of intimacy that existed between him and his wife for years:

> The two New York years in which she withheld from me all kisses on the mouth, withheld these quietly and steadily and without complaint, averting even her eyes whenever mine sought them out in emotion, all the while cultivating a dutiful domesticity and maternal ethic that armored her in blamelessness, leaving me with no way to approach her, no way to find fault or feelings, waiting for me to lose heart, to put away my most human wants and expectations, to carry my burdens secretly, she not once in my mourning mentioned my mother, even that time when I wept in the kitchen and dropped a bottle of beer on the floor out of pure sorrow. She merely wiped the floor with paper towels and said nothing, brushing her free hand against my shoulder blade – my shoulder blade! – as she carried the soaked paper to the trash can, never holding me fast, refraining not out of lack of humanity but out of fear of being drawn into a request for further tenderness... (pages 127- 128).

Thus, Rachel not only withheld from gestures common to those in love, but also emotional intimacy. For fear of intimacy, Rachel did not even extend the common courtesy of commiserating in her husband's sorrow at the death of his mother. She maintained the decorum that was businesslike, which put Hans off from emotionally approaching her. But what Hans did not realize was that Rachel, his wife, was feeling the same thing; a need to be loved. Rachel once shouted at Hans, "I don't need to be provided for! I'm a lawyer! I make two hundred and fifty thousand dollars a year! I need to be loved!" (page 128). But when Rachel needed love or an emotional response, instead of hugging her or telling her that he loved her, Hans quietly picked up the baby and took him for a crawl in the hotel corridor. Hans ran away when his wife needed him emotionally, and Rachel was emotionally absent when Hans needed her love. They were the same in terms of being emotionally absent in New York, which caused the marital separation.

The marital troubles, emotional distance, and the separation are, in essence, blamed on New York City and American capitalism, which is portrayed as evil in the novel, *Netherland*. Although Rachel made $250,000 per year as a lawyer in New York City, her money-centered job left her exhausted and extremely tired. When Hans came back after taking baby Jake for a crawl to talk with her, his wife Rachel had fallen fast asleep. Hans the narrator describes, "Afterwards washed the baby's filthy hands and soft filthy knees, and thought about what his wife had said, and saw the truth in her words and an opening, and decided to make another attempt at kindness, and at nine o'clock, with the baby finally drowsy in his cot, came with a full heart back to his wife to find her asleep, as usual, and beyond waking" (pages 128-129). Thus, the rigor of the American capitalist system is blamed to a large extent on the breakdown of the marriage of Rachel and Hans. The rigorous system produces intense fatigue and lack of emotional and mental space for intimacy and love.

Like Rachel, Hans was a victim of New York City's American capitalism; Hans prided himself in making a lot of money, but he was deprived of the human factor. When Hans meets Martin Casey, Rachel's lover during the marital separation, in London and sees him playing with Jake who "leaped on Martin's back and began pawing at him" (page 225), Hans is filled with jealousy. When Martin says, "Business is good" (page 225), Hans thinks to himself, "Oh yeah? I wanted to say. Get back to me when you're grossing ten thousand dollars per working day, asshole" (page 225). Certainly, whatever Martin made could not compare to Hans' earnings in New York City's American capitalism, and Hans tried to find solace in that. But the fact is, Hans' son wasn't playing with Hans, and Hans' wife chose someone else. While making money in American capitalism, Hans lost everything that mattered to him as a human being.

Another good illustration of how American capitalism had victimized Hans is found in the scene where Hans celebrates his professional accomplishment, only to find that his personal life is falling apart; in a sense, it was New York City's American capitalism that had destroyed what was truly dear to Hans. Hans was an equities analysts for M---, a merchant bank with a gargantuan brokerage operation. In fact, such a bank embodied American capitalism and New York City.

Hans van den Broek was among the best. In fact, *Institutional Investor* ranked him fourth in his sector, which was a climb of six spaces from the previous year. Hans analyzed large-cap oil and gas stocks, and inside the industry, Hans had "the beginnings of a reputation as a guru" (page 26). To celebrate the achievement, Hans took his coworkers out to a bar in Midtown. After being a little drunk, Hans returned home to his wife and child. His son Jake was asleep and his wife was on the bed, from which she was looking at the window. Hans realizes the uselessness of his professional achievement in light of his marriage falling apart; his wife Rachel had declared her intent to leave for London with Jake that week. Being a bit drunk, Hans musters the courage to tell Rachel what he really wants: "Rachel, I said quietly, it's very simple: I'm coming with you. Still in my coat, I knelt beside her. We'll all go, I said. I'll collect my bonus and then we'll head off together, as a family. London would be just fine. Anywhere would be fine. Tuscany, Tehran, it doesn't matter. OK? Let's do it. Let's have an adventure. Let's live" (pages 27-28). Of course, Hans wanted to emphasize that it was his family which was important, but being a little drunk, Hans came off sounding flippant. Hans assumed that there was adventure involved, rather than hard work to make marriage work and a family to be together.

Netherland by Joseph O'Neill & President Barak Obama's AMERICA

Realizing that Hans did not understand, Rachel tells her husband directly, "You've abandoned me, Hans. …. I don't know why, but you've left me to fend for myself. And I can't fend for myself. I just can't" (page 29). Hans had been working so hard to advance himself professionally that he had forgotten to be there for his wife and the kids. The only time he speaks honestly with his wife is when he is drunk, celebrating his professional accomplishments. The contrast between Hans drinking in celebration with his coworkers and Hans' wife Rachel at home with their baby Jake is stark. In a sense, the scene is meant to be an indictment of the problems of American capitalism, which centralizes professional advancement and spending social time with coworkers and minimizes family life. Hans was a victim because he was caught in the midst of the excitement of American capitalism and even made impressive accomplishments by the standards of American capitalism, but that accomplishment was the very reason why Hans lost what was dear to him, his wife and his child.

Hans realized the trap of American capitalism and tried to make his escape through cricket, a sport which most Americans have never even heard of. Hans describes, "Whenever possible I took my lunch in Bryant Park, because in Bryant Park I could lie down on grass and inhale the scent of cricket, and look up at the sky and see a cricketer's blue sky, and close my eyes and feel on my skin the heat that coats a fielder" (page 172). Hans valued his cricket time as sacred, a time separated from his work and American capitalism. Thus, when Hans was on the club's fundraising committee, Hans lied about raising $5,000 from some "crazy" Indian guys at work; the truth was that Hans had written the check for $5,000 himself, because he wanted to keep his work separate from cricket, which he treasured. Hans describes, "There were Indian guys at work but they weren't crazy, and even if they had been crazy I wouldn't have involved them in this part of my life, whose separateness was part of its preciousness" (page 173). For Hans, cricket was sacred and an escape. And in his sacred escape, Hans meets Chuck and develops strong friendship with him, which in a sense is sacred, since it is based on cricket, which becomes the most sacred element in Hans' life in New York City.

Rachel misunderstands and assumes that Chuck was Hans's social experiment of a kind. Hans describes Rachel's notions: "She has accused me of exoticizing Chuck Ramkissoon, of giving him a pass, of failing to grant him a respectful measure of distrust, of perpetrating a white man's infantilizing elevation of a black man" (page 166). In other words, according to Rachel, Hans was patronizing Chuck in a type of racial patronizing.

This accusation of Rachel that Hans is patronizing Chuck and "giving him a pass" is interesting, because it does not jive with Hans' own reflections during his encounters with Chuck Ramkissoon. If anything, Hans is hypersuspicious of Chuck and questions his motives, perhaps more than would be necessary in a friendship. From the very start, Hans doubted Chuck's motives: "My instinct was to keep him at a distance, at that distance, certainly, that we introduce between ourselves and those we suspect of neediness. I was wondering, for example, when he was going to ask me for money for his cricket scheme. But I was drawn to Chuck" (page 102). Even though Hans liked Chuck, Hans was hypersuspicious of him. Even after the friendship had blossomed, Hans doubted Chuck. When Chuck gives Hans driving lessons with his Cadillac, Hans doubts Chuck's motivation. Hans reflects, "I understood, now, the point of my driving lessons. It gave Chuck a measure of cover, maybe even prestige, to have a respectable-looking white man chauffeuring him while he ran around collecting bets all over Brooklyn" (page 171). It was Hans who saw himself as superior to Chuck. Hans was fixated on his whiteness, and suspected his colored friend, whom he, in essence, considered inferior. He thought that all that colored people are wont to do was to use white people. Hans did not give Chuck the benefit of the doubt. What triggered this train of thought for Hans was the fact that Chuck took care of some of his shady business, while they were driving together. Hans did not need to think that Chuck was manipulating the situation for his own ends. If Hans were giving Chuck the benefit of the doubt, Hans could have thought that Chuck was nice enough to help him with the driving test, and since there is only so much time in a day, Chuck took care of some business, while they were out driving.

The fact that after Chuck had helped Hans prepare for the driving test, he brought Hans to a cricket field and played cricket with him and worked together to better cricket further proves that Chuck was motivated primarily by friendship. Hans describes: "Once a weekend, then, Chuck became my driving mentor, as he put it – thereby casting me as poor Telemachus – and in return I became his assistant groundskeeper, because our motorized promenades invariably ended with cutting or rolling or watering his cricket field" (page 152). It is important to note that Chuck Ramkissoon did not make Hans work on the cricket field alone. By Hans' own admission, Hans became his "assistant," which means that Chuck did a lot of the work primarily. They both worked on something they both enjoyed and loved; namely, cricket. Besides, more often than not, Hans and Chuck played cricket after Chuck helped with Hans' driving test preparation. Hans describes,

> We walked together to the field's center. This was how we ended each of our sessions of groundsmanship: by whacking a dozen balls to the edge of the field and studying the consistency of each sector of the field. We were making progress. The outfield was getting quicker and truer. In accordance with our routine, I took the bat and with one-handed underarm strokes scattered the balls in every direction. We circled the field together, picking up the balls dotted around the field like markers of hours" (page 171).

If anything, this description makes it clear that Chuck was a better friend to Hans and did not deserve Hans' overly critical

Netherland by Joseph O'Neill & President Barak Obama's AMERICA

suspicion. For one, Chuck let Hans hit the balls. As anyone who ever played sports knows, that is the fun part. Picking up the ball that had been hit is not the fun part. Chuck allowed Hans to hit the ball, and then Chuck and Hans picked up the ball, together. Clearly, Chuck was the selfless friend. Furthermore, after their fun time together in the cricket field, Chuck went out of his way to drive Hans wherever he wanted. Chuck could have just told Hans to take public transportation or a taxi. Hans does not even realize Chuck's kind nature, when Hans describes, "Afterwards, as was usual, Chuck drove me to wherever it was I was playing that day – Baisley Pond Park, perhaps, or Fort Tilden Park, or Kissena Corridor Park, or Sound View Park. Our field and those fields were in one continuum of heat and greenness" (pages 171-172). It seems like the friendship was focused on Hans, to make him happy. With all the sacrifices that Chuck made for Hans and all his efforts at friendship, Hans should not but have realized that Chuck was his friend.

In a sense, Chuck Ramkissoon was not only Hans' friend but his savior of sorts. Hans admits that Chuck is his savior in a way, when he states, "I had troubles of my own, and Chuck's companionship functioned as an asylum" (page 135). Chuck's friendship gave Hans meaning in life. Furthermore, it provided him with fun activities. Obviously, there were the enjoyable cricket activities.

Also, Chuck invited Hans to fun activities, such as the 2003 Annual Gala of the Association of New York Cricket Leagues, which was held at the Elegant Antun's, Springfield Boulevard, Queens. And Chuck introduced to Hans to his friends, an Indian businessman named Prashanth Ramachandran, a retired Shri Lankan pathologist named Dr. Flavian Seem, and two Guyanese brothers who imported burnt sugar, almond essence, sorrel syrup, and baby Edam cheese, and a young elegant woman in a silver frock, named Avalon. Chuck was so worried about Hans having fun that Chuck arranged to have Hans dance with Avalon. Hans describes the dance: "I danced with Avalon. That is, I clumsily moved around in her vicinity, glimpsing in the grins of those nearby the encouragement usually reserved for children. I was the only white person present, and reinforcing a stereotype. Avalon herself politely smiled and laughed and gave no sign of noticing my lumbersomeness..." (page 140). Chuck was always concerned about Hans, because Chuck was his true friend. In a sense, Chuck was a savior who saved Hans from the monotony of his life as an equities analyst. Hans led a deeply boring life as an equities analyst. Hans describes the monotony of what he does, even by the standards of the business world:

> The business world is densely margined by dreamers, men, almost invariably, whose longing selves willingly submit to the enchantment of projections and pie charts and crisply totted numbers, who toy and toy for years, like novelists, with the same leaf of documents, who slip out of bed in the middle of the night to pitch to a pajama'd reflection in a windowpane. I've never been open to the fantastical aspect of business. I'm an analyst – a bystander. I lack entrepreneurial wistfulness (page 103).

Chuck Ramkissoon, in a sense, saved Hans from a life devoid of meaning and excitement. Chuck is that kind of a good guy who is good to all. Thus, Chuck stands in stark contrast to his business partner, Mikhail Abelsky.

In contrast to the selfish and greedy Abelsky, Chuck Ramkissoon was a generous individual. Chuck helped Hans with driving practice, so he could get a driver's license, and helped him to enjoy cricket. The fact that Chuck took the leadership role time and time again, even on the social level, further supports the idea that Abelsky had lied about Chuck being his employee. Chuck was a leader not only vis-à-vis Abelsky, he was so in reference to Hans, who was a successful equities analyst. In other words, Chuck was a highly competent individual and a leader. Besides being generous, Chuck

Ramkissoon was a very open person. Chuck Ramkissoon introduces Hans to his wife and invited him to breakfast at his house, which consisted of "an exotic pink mush" (page 158), which was saltfish, while Chuck's wife Anne prepared stew chicken for their church pastor's birthday celebration.

Furthermore, Chuck Ramkissoon was a hard worker. Chuck Ramkissoon arrived in the USA with his wife right after marrying her at the age of twenty-five. And Chuck Ramkissoon started working on "the first day of his supposed honeymoon" (page 133). Chuck describes his hard work at the beginning of his immigrant life in the USA: "I had a cousin – actually, the friend of a cousin – taking care of me. Painting, plastering, demolition, cement work, roofing, you name it, I did it. I'd come home to Brownville with this white face and grit on my hands. I couldn't wash it out, you know. For years, my hands were always dirty" (page 133). Chuck Ramkissoon embodies the hardworking American immigrant who is the ideal immigrant, and readers are left rooting for him, so that he could fulfill his American dream. Chuck Ramkissoon tells Hans about his first break:

> Then I got my big break. It was my wife, actually, who got it for me. …. She was a babysitter for this high-end Manhattan couple. They needed work done to their summer place on the Island. I gained their confidence and I took the job. It was my first job as chief contractor. Then I did their new apartment on Beach Street. Soon everybody else in the building wanted me as well. They liked me (page 133).

Although the readers excitedly follow Chuck Ramkissoon's exciting break and his search for the American dream, at the back of their minds, the readers know that Chuck Ramkissoon would fail to achieve his American dream and end up murdered. In fact, the failure of the American dream in the current

Netherland by Joseph O'Neill & President Barak Obama's AMERICA

American capitalistic system for hard-working individuals may be seen as a theme of this novel, which paints American capitalism in the most negative light. American capitalism is the problem. After all, the story begins with the narrator in England, having returned there after abandoning New York City, and the story ends at that precisely the same point.

The novel works hard to build the image of Chuck Ramkissoon as a hardworking immigrant who wants to fulfill the American dream, in order to highlight the danger of American capitalism, as represented by New York City. Furthermore, Mikhail Abelsky is set up as a type of Shylock the Jew, who ends the dream of a good guy, Chuck, just the same way Shylock the Jew tried to destroy the good guy, Antonio, who wanted to help his friend Bassanio in a self-sacrificial way.

Although Antonio the Christian in *The Merchant of Venice* could escape the taking of the pound of flesh by a Jew, Chuck Ramkissoon the Christian in *Netherland* fails to do so. The book title, *Netherland*, is significant in this regard. Netherland was one of the first countries to offer Jews safety and protection, when the wave of persecution of Jews started in Europe in the late Middle Ages. In 1581, the Declaration of Independence (Act of Abjuration) was issued by the United Provinces, which guaranteed religious toleration of Jews in the Article 13 of Unie van Utrecht. As a result, Jews from Portugal and Spain, which persecuted them, turned to Holland. This book is using irony to highlight what happens to Christians in a capitalism in which Shylocks are protected, and the ramification of that system is the death of a Christian businessman who becomes susceptible. Thus, *The Merchant of Venice* and *Netherland* share a common motif.

Chuck Ramkissoon, who is not a white collar migrant, perhaps better represents the failure of the American dream and the evils of American capitalism. Chuck Ramkissoon is a dark-skinned Trinidadian of Indian descent, who wants to make it big in the USA, so he embarks on small business ventures. He recognizes his own limitation as a colored man, and recruits a Russian Jew to be the visage of his small company operations.

Netherland by Joseph O'Neill & President Barak Obama's AMERICA

Chuck Ramkissoon believes that he has everything covered. His partner would lend him his white face and Jewishness, which are currency in certain parts of New York, and in exchange, Chuck Ramkissoon makes him a partner and enriches him. When Chuck Ramkissoon is murdered, the suspicion of the narrative is on his white Jewish partner, who has everything to gain from Chuck Ramkissoon's death. Chuck's companies were in the name of the white Russian Jew, because Chuck Ramkissoon thought that would help his business. Chuck took Abelsky everywhere, teaching him the tricks of the trade. The suspicion is that Abelsky, after learning all the tricks of the trade, did away with Chuck Ramkisson.

Like *The Merchant of Venice*, *Netherland* portrays Judaism in a negative light. In *Netherland*, Judaism is portrayed as corrupt and ridiculous. For instance, when Chuck Ramkissoon wants to get the kosher certification for his sushi restaurant, his Jewish partner, Abelsky, obtains the kosher certification for him. Chuck Ramkissoon brags to Hans, the narrator of the story, "I have a Jewish partner who has the confidence of the rabbi. Makes things a lot easier" (page 56). Chuck makes it sound like it's the Jewish connection that matters more than the content of religion. Thus, Abelsky becomes like a middlemen in a business transaction, and receiving the kosher certification is a type of a business transaction.

Netherland portrays Jewish kosher laws as ridiculous. Chuck Ramkissoon spends much time to describe the kosher laws that pertain to sushi, and the readers are left thinking how ridiculous it all is. Chuck states:

> But I tell you, getting kosher certification is a tough business. Tougher than the pharmaceuticals business, I like to say. You wouldn't believe the problems that come up. Earlier this year we had some trouble with seahorses. .... You know how you check nori, the seaweed you wrap the sushi in? You

> examine it over a light box, like an X-ray. And they found seahorse infestation in our supplier's seaweed. And seahorses are not kosher. Neither are shrimps and eels and octopus and squid. Only fish with scales and fins are kosher. But not all fish with fins have scales…. And sometimes what you think are scales are in fact bony protrusions. Bony protrusions do not qualify as scales. No, sir. ….. What are we left with? Halibut, salmon, red snapper, mackerel, mahi-mahi, tuna – but only certain kinds of tuna. Which ones? Albacore, skipjack, yellowfin. …. What about fish eggs, roe? …. The eggs of kosher fish are generally shaped differently from nonkosher fish. Also, they tend to be red, whereas nonkosher are black. Then there are issues with rice, issues with vinegar. Sushi vinegar will often contain nonkosher ingredients or will be made using a nonkosher process. There are issues with worms in the flesh of the fish, with utensils, with storage, with filling, with freezing, with sauces, with the broths and oils you pack the fish in. Every aspect of the process is difficult. It's a painstaking business, I'm telling you (pages 56-57).

The detailed description of Jewish kosher rules makes Judaism look ridiculous. Since kosher laws are fundamental to Judaism, this can be seen as a direct attack on Judaism.

Such attack on Judaism's kosher tradition can be found in *The Merchant of Venice* by Shakespeare. In *The Merchant of Venice*, kosher laws are used to show Jews as antisocial. It is because of the kosher laws that Shylock refuses to eat with Gentiles. In *The Merchant of Venice*, when Bassanio invites Shylock to a meal in a gesture of friendship, Shylock replies, "Yes, to smell pork; to eat of the habitation which your prophet the Nazarite conjured the devil into. I will buy with you, sell with you, talk with you, walk with you, and so following; but I will not eat with you, drink with you, nor pray with you" (Act 1, Scene 3). Thus, Shakespeare portrays Judaism as fundamentally anti-social in the Gentile world. Chuck Ramkissoon's description of the kosher laws pertaining to sushi conjures up the same kind of idea that Judaism is incompatible with the Gentile world.

The key signifier of "tribe" in *Netherland* indicates that the association is not accidental. A key signifier is a literary device used to trigger the audience to mental or physical action. A key signifier involves the use of a word or phrase that triggers either a communal collective memory in events or in literature that has a particular significance. The key signifier is intended then to initiate a second trigger of prompting the intended audience to mental or physical action.[257]

In *Netherland*, after a week or so after the kosher lecture by Chuck Ramkissoon, Hans receives a note by Chuck Ramkissoon that states: "Dear Hans, You know that you are a member of the first tribe of New York, excepting of course the Red Indians. Here is something you might like. Best wishes, Chuck Ramkissoon" (page 58). The "tribe" in the note is meant to trigger the intelligent readers as to the literary use of "tribe" in *The Merchant of Venice*. Thus, the key signifier of "tribe" can be seen as meant for highly literate segment of the readers of the book. However, the literary are not the only intended audience for the key signifier. Anyone who is a Christian who goes to a Christian church knows that when the word "tribe" is used, it is used in association with the Israelite tribes of the Old Testament. It is natural for Christians to make the corollary association to "Jews." Thus, the key signifier of "tribe" (especially "the first tribe") is meant for Christians who go to church and read the Bible.

---

[257] For a fuller discussion of the literary device of the key signifier, read Heerak Christian Kim, *Key Signifier as Literary Device: Its Definition and Function in Literature and Media* (Lewiston: The Edwin Mellon Press, 2006).

In *The Merchant of Venice*, "tribe" is certainly used to refer to the Jews. In *The Merchant of Venice*, Shylock, the religious Jew, uses the world "tribe" to refer to himself and his group in his thoughts against Antonio, a Christian:

> [*Aside*] How like a fawning publican[258] he looks!
> I hate him for he is a Christian;
> But more that in low simplicity
> He lends out money gratis and brings down
> The rate of usance here with us in Venice.
> If I can catch him once upon the hip,
> I will feed fat the ancient grudge[259] I bear him.
> He hates our sacred nation;[260] and he rails,
> Even there where merchants most do congregate,[261]
> On me, my bargains, and my well-won thrift,
> Which he calls interest. Cursed be my tribe,
> If I forgive him! (Act 1, Scene 3).

---

[258] "Publican" can be seen as a key signifier, since Jesus was accused of eating with "publicans and sinners" in the Gospels (Mark 2:16) by the Pharisees and Jewish scribes. Antonio, being "publican," can be seen as a friend of Jesus, whom Shylock the Jew hates. This fits in light of the rest of Shylock's thinking in Shakespeare's *The Merchant of Venice*.

[259] Ancient grudge refers to the Jewish grudge against Jesus of Nazareth as described in the Gospels.

[260] One of the reasons why Shylock the Jew hates Antonio is that Antonio is anti-Zionist. Thus, "nation" is a key signifier that triggers the collective memory about "nation" as used in the context of Jewish leadership's decision to kill Jesus of Nazareth. One of the reasons offered by the High Priest of the Jerusalem for killing Jesus of Nazareth was for Jewish nationalism (Zionism) interests. See John 11:47-54.

[261] Merchants congregating is a key signifier meant to trigger the collective memory of Jesus of Nazareth railing against the merchants in the Jerusalem Temple (Matthew 21:13). Jesus of Nazareth accuses Jewish merchants of having made the Jerusalem Temple into a "den of thieves." Shylock the banker is described as a type of a thief, thus Shakespeare's use of the key signifier is strategic.

Shylock calls down curse on his tribe. "Cursed be my tribe" reminds the readers of the curse that Jews called upon themselves according to the Gospel account of the trial of Jesus of Nazareth. In Matthew 27:25, the Jewish crowd described as crying out, "His blood be on us and our children."

It is significant that Shakespeare's key signifier of "tribe" recalls the biblical text of Jews calling curses upon themselves. Such sentiment is captured by the key signifier of "tribe" in *Netherland*. The piece of note that Chuck Ramkissoon wrote Hans contains the concept of genocide. For some Christians, the holocaust of the Jews is seen as the fulfillment of the curse that the Jews had called upon themselves in Matthew 27:25. The note of Chuck Ramkissoon contains "Red Indians" which remind the readers of genocide. Again, the note containing the key signifier of "tribe" in *Netherland* reads: "Dear Hans, You know that you are a member of the first tribe of New York, excepting of course the Red Indians. Here is something you might like. Best wishes, Chuck Ramkissoon" (page 58). In a sense, there is a parallel between the passage containing "tribe" in *The Merchant of Venice* and the passage containing the key signifier of "tribe" in *Netherland*; they both point to the Jewish tribe and to their curse upon themselves, which some post-holocaust Christians describes as having been fulfilled in Hitler's genocide of the Jews.

The key signifier in Netherland can be seen as a complex key signifier because there has to be corollary associations, but they are not too difficult to make since because Red Indians suffered genocide in America and Jews suffered genocide in Europe. In other words, the complex key signifier allows the association to be made easily. Furthermore, the part of the long passage describing kosher rules related to sushi in *Netherland* is separated from the note containing the key signifier of "tribe" by one significant piece of information: "CHUCK CRICKET, INC. Chuck Ramkissoon, President" (page 58). In the truly English fashion, the key signifier is expected to undergo a type of "cricket element." In other words, just like baseball, which is a game that takes place in a few hours, and cricket takes place over several days, readers are expected to patiently sift through the complex key signifier as if it were cricket and takes a lot of time. This idea is supported by the novel itself.

In *Netherland*, "cricket" is used in meaningful ways. Cricket is tied to American culture. There is the idea with symbolic significance that cricket is fundamentally American but it has lost its purpose. In an email that Chuck Ramkissoon sent out, Chuck writes: "Cricket was first modern team sport in America. It came before baseball and football" (page 101).

In a sense, "cricket" can be seen as a metaphor for Christianity. Christianity was the first organized religion, or social institution, in America, before any other socio-religious institution took hold, such as secularism or other religions. However, Christianity especially in New York City is seen as an immigrant "thing." Many white churches are empty or closed down and ethnic churches are thriving. Chuck Ramkissoon describes this association in symbolic terms: "So it is wrong to see cricket in America as most people see it i.e. an immigrant sport. It is a bona fide American pastime and should be regarded as such. All those who have attempted to 'introduce' cricket to the American public have failed to understand this. Cricket is already in the American DNA" (page 102). There is a symbolic criticism of those who try to evangelize the Americans (or "whites" since most minority immigrant ethnic groups call whites, "Americans") with the Christian Gospel, who often pit themselves against American pop culture or American society; rather, Chuck Ramkissoon symbolically reminds the readers that Christianity is the skeleton of the American society. It is "in the blood," so to speak, in America. In other words, through the lens of cricket, or Christianity, key signifiers could be better understood. Thus, in a sense, readers are expected to play "cricket" to understand the meaning behind the text.

Obviously, the key signifier is employed to make the identification between Shylock the Jew in *The Merchant of Venice* and Mikhail Abelsky in *Netherland*. In both narratives, the Jewish individual is the villain of the story, although that is more explicitly stated in *The Merchant of Venice*.

The fundamental difference between the two narratives, of course, is that in *The Merchant of Venice*, Shylock the Jew is outsmarted and defeated. But this was possible because the society in *The Merchant of Venice* is a Christian society with Christian justices, which provided protection for Christians from stated Jewish villainy. In contrast, the present-day New York City is not seen as a Christian city or a place conducive to protection of Christians. In such American capitalism, a Christian businessman, Chuck Ramkissoon, becomes vulnerable, and loses his "pound of flesh" to his Jewish partner, Mikhail Abelsky. In a sense, both of the narratives have a Jewish character to highlight the evils of the system or the weaknesses of the system that could be manipulated.

To a large extent, the character of Mikhail Abelsky should be seen as a type of Shylock the Jew in *The Merchant of Venice* and as a form of literary exercise that is applied in the context of modern-day America. Like *The Merchant of Venice*, *Netherland* should be seen as striving for a type of historicity in the context of the contemporary reality as pertaining to Jews and the popular perception of Jews. As literature often tries to understand the socio-political environment and the motivations of people in that environment, *Netherland* by Joseph O'Neill should be seen as a superb literary work that succeeds in such a literary exercise, as *The Merchant of Venice* by William Shakespeare.

Bibliography

Amidon, Stephen. "Netherland by Joseph O'Neill." *The Sunday Times*. June 8, 2008 (http://entertainment.timesonline.co.uk/tol/arts_and_entertainment/books/fiction/article4074760.ece)

Anthony, Michael. *Historical Dictionary of Trinidad and Tobago*. Lanham: The Scarecrow Press, Inc., 1997.

Anthony, Michael. *Profile Trinidad: A Historical Survey from the Discovery to 1900*. London: Macmillan, 1975.

Asim, Jabari. *What Obama Means ... for Our Culture, Our Politics, Our Future*. New York: William Morrow, 2009.

Balz, Dan, and Haynes Johnson. *The Battle for America 2008: The Story of an Extraordinary Election*. New York: Viking, 2009.

Beinart, Peter. "Shrinking the War on Terrorism." *Time* (Vol. 174, No. 23) December 14, 2009, pp. 42-45.

Borde, Pierre-Gustave-Louis. *The History of Trinidad under the Spanish Government (Volume 1): 1492-1622*. Translated by James Alva Bain. Port-of-Spain: Paria Publishing Co. Ltd., 1982.

Brereton, Bridget. *Race Relations in Colonial Trinidad 1870-1900*. Cambridge: Cambridge University Press, 1979.

Burke, Monte. "Downshift," in *Forbes*, Volume 185, Number 7 (April 25, 2010), page 63-66.

De Verteuil, Anthony. *The Years of Revolt: Trinidad 1881-1888.* Port-of-Spain: Paria Publishing Co. Ltd., 1984.

Economist, The. "Betrayed by Obama: Some of the New President's Most Arden Supporters Already Feel Let Down." *The Economist.* January 22, 2009 (http://www.economist.com/world/united-states/displaystory.cfm?story_id=E1_TNJRSVDV)

Garner, Dwight. "The Ashes." *The New York Times.* May 18, 2008 (http://www.nytimes.com/2008/05/18/books/review/Garner-t.html)

Hirsh, Michael. "Memo to President Obama: Never Mind Iraq. Just End the 'War on Terror.'" *Newsweek.* February 21, 2008 (http://www.newsweek.com/id/114385)

Hustvedt, Siri. "After the Fall." *The Washington Post.* June 1, 2008 (http://www.washingtonpost.com/wp-dyn/content/article/2008/05/29/AR2008052903362.html)

Johnson, Dennis W. (Editor). *Campaigning for President 2008: Strategy and Tactics, New Voices and New Techniques.* New York: Routledge, 2009.

Johnson, Kim. *Descendants of the Dragon: The Chinese in Trinidad 1806-2006.* Kingston: Ian Randle Publishers, 2006.

Jones, Beth. "A Cricket-Playing Dutchman in New York." *The Telegraph.* June 15, 2008 (http://www.telegraph.co.uk/culture/books/fictionreviews/3554439/A-cricket-playing-Dutchman-in-New-York.html)

Kaufman, Robert G. *In Defense of the Bush Doctrine*. Lexington: The University Press of Kentucky, 2007.

Kelley, Colleen Elizabeth. *Post-9/11 American Presidential Rhetoric: A Study of Protofascist Discourse*. Lanham: Lexington Books, 2007.

Kellner, Douglas. *From 9/11 to Terror War: The Dangers of the Bush Legacy*. Lanham: Rowman & Littlefield Publishers, Inc., 2003.

Kim, Heerak Christian. *Key Signifier as Literary Device: Its Definition and Function in Literature and Media*. Lewiston: The Edwin Mellon Press, 2006.

Kitfield, James. *War & Destiny: How the Bush Revolution in Foreign and Military Affairs Redefined American Power*. Washington, DC: Potomac Books, Inc., 2005.

Klein, Joe. "A President and His War." *Time* (Vol. 174, No. 23) December 14, 2009, pp. 36-40.

Kunkel, Benjamin. "Men in White." *London Review of Books*. Vol. 30 No. 14 · 17 July 2008 (http://www.lrb.co.uk/v30/n14/benjamin-kunkel/men-in-white)

La Guerre, John Gaffar (Editor). *Calcutta to Caroni: The East Indians of Trinidad*. London: Longman, 1974.

Luke, Learie B. *Identity and Secession in the Caribbean: Tobago versus Trinidad, 1889-1980*. Jamaica: University of the West Indies Press, 2007.

Lustick, Ian S. *Trapped in* the War on Terror. Philadelphia: University of Pennsylvania Press, 2006.

Netherland **by Joseph O'Neill & President Barak Obama's AMERICA**

MacDonald, Scott B. *Trinidad and Tobago: Democracy and Development in the Caribbean.* New York: Praeger, 1986.

Magid, Alvin. *Urban Nationalism: A Study of Political Development in Trinidad.* Gainesville: University of Florida Press, 1988.

Malik, Yogendra K. *East Indians in Trinidad: A Study in Minority Politics.* London: Oxford University Press, 1971.

Maury, Laurel. "Often the Watcher in Want of Life 'Netherland' is Perceptive but Alienating." *Los Angeles Times.* May 27, 2008 (http://articles.latimes.com/2008/may/27/entertainment/et-book27)

Mayer, Jane. *The Dark Side: The Inside Story of How the War on Terror Turned into a War on American Ideals.* New York: Doubleday, 2008.

Morris, Dick, and Eileen McGann. *Catastrophe: How Obama, Congress, and the Special Interest Are Transforming ... a Slump into a Crash, Freedom into Socialism, and a Disaster into a Catastrophe ... and How to Fight Back.* New York: Harper, 2009.

Mueller, John. *Overblown: How Politicians and the Terrorism Industry Inflate National Security Threats, and Why We Believe Them.* New York: Free Press, 2006.

O'Hagan, Sean. "He's Got Something to Declare." *The Observer.* June 1, 2008 (http://www.guardian.co.uk/books/2008/jun/01/fiction1/print)

O'Neill, Joseph. *Netherland.* New York: Vintage Books, 2008.

Obama, Barack. *The Audacity of Hope: Thoughts on Reclaiming the American Dream.* New York: Vintage Books, 2006.

Obama, Barack. *Change We Can Believe In: Barack Obama's Plan to Renew America's Promise.* New York: Three Rivers Press, 2008.

Oxaal, Ivar. *Black Intellectuals Come to Power: The Rise of Creole Nationalism in Trinidad & Tobago.* Cambridge: Schenkman Publishing Company, Inc., 1968.

Pedersen, Carl. *Obama's America.* Edinburgh: Edinburgh University Press, 2009.

Rogak, Lisa (Editor). *Barack Obama in His Own Words.* Philadelphia: Running Press, 2009.

Ryan, Selwyn D. *Race and Nationalism in Trinidad and Tobago: A Study of Decolonization in a Multiracial Society.* Toronto: University of Toronto Press, 1972.

Savage, Charlie. "Obama's War on Terror May Resemble Bush's in Some Areas." *The New York Times.* February 17, 2009 (http://www.nytimes.com/2009/02/18/us/politics/18policy.html)

Shakespeare, William. *The Merchant of Venice.* New York: Dover Publications, Inc., 1995.

Shanahan, Timothy (Editor). *Philosophy 9/11: Thinking about the War on Terrorism.* Chicago: Open Court, 2005.

Netherland by Joseph O'Neill & President Barak Obama's AMERICA

Singh, Kelvin. *Race and Class Struggles in a Colonial State: Trinidad 1917-1945*. Calgary: University of Calgary Press, 1994.

Smith, Ed. "Netherland by Joseph O'Neill." *The Times*. June 20, 2008 (http://entertainment.timesonline.co.uk/tol/arts_and_entertainment/books/fiction/article4178788.ece)

Smith, Zadie. "Two Paths for the Novel." *The New York Review of Books*. Vol. 55, No. 18, November 20, 2008 (http://www.nybooks.com/articles/22083)

Tayler, Christopher. "Christopher Tayler finds Joseph O'Neill on a sticky wicket with his novel of New York cricketers, Netherland." *The Guardian*. June 14, 2008 (http://www.guardian.co.uk/books/2008/jun/14/saturdayreviewsfeatres.guardianreview7/print)

Von Lovenberg, Felicitas. "Joseph O'Neill: 'Niederland': Die letzten Bürger von Pompeji leben in New York." *Frankfurter Allgemeine*. March 6, 2009 (http://www.faz.net/s/Rub48A3E114E72543C4938ADBB2DCEE2108/Doc~EAE9153383D4D4B9F9057E1A31AE5A882~ATpl~Ecommon~Scontent.html)

Williams, Eric. *History of the People of Trinidad and Tobago*. Port-of-Spain: PNM Publishing Co. Ltd., 1962.

Wood, Donald. *Trinidad in Transition: The Years after Slavery*. London: Oxford University Press, 1968.

Wood, James. "Beyond a Boundary." *The New Yorker*. May 26, 2006 (http://www.newyorker.com/arts/critics/books/2008/05/26/080526crbo_books_wood?printable=true)

Young, Virginia Heyer. *Becoming West Indian: Culture, Self, and Nation in St. Vincent.* Washington: Smithsonian Institution Press, 1993.

Zipp, Yvonne. "Netherland." The Christian Science Monitor. July 11, 2008 (http://www.csmonitor.com/Books/Book-Reviews/2008/0711/netherland)

www.ingramcontent.com/pod-product-compliance
Lightning Source LLC
Chambersburg PA
CBHW022106160426
43198CB00008B/367